Zippoo

Zippoo

Ventures of a Curious Child

Charlotte Giovanella Fullam

For Katie

Family

Annetta Giovanella: Nonna

Luigi Giovanella: Nonno

Bancroft Davis: Grandpa Davis

Charlotte Davis: Grandma Davis

Alice Davis Giovanella: Alse, Allie, Mummy, Mum

Renato Giovanella: Rinardo, Daddy, Dad, Nardo, Nawdo, Joe

Italo Giovanella: Uncle Iggy

Charlotte Giovanella: Zip, Zippy, Spindleshanks, Zippoo

Katharine Giovanella: Kathy, Kath

Mary Louise Giovanella: Louise, Lou

Katharine Foote Raffy: Aunt Katharine,
Rev (rhymes with nerve), Revy

Henri Raffy: Uncle Henri, Manny

Gerry Davis: Uncle Gerry
(pronounced with hard G like Gary)

Ophelia Mae Hadlock: Gram Hadlock, Gram, Grammy

Table of Contents

Charlotte Fullam

Journey's End

Preface

As the eldest of three daughters, I was raised by my parents in rural Maine in the 1940s and early '50s. They had the support of my godmother, Rev and her husband, Manny, a French army veteran of WWI, not to mention a cast of other characters, many of whom you'll encounter in the pages that follow.

That all this came to pass defies belief.

Picture, if you can, my mother: a sophisticated, but frequently depressed young woman, daughter of a prominent Boston family, marrying a bright, handsome, musical son of Italian immigrants, when she was eighteen and he was twenty-three. Their backgrounds were so different it's surprising and commendable that they lived together, with their ups and downs, for 68 years.

As newlyweds, Alice and Nardo moved to rural Porter, Maine where Rev and Manny (with the help of skilled neighbors) had restored a dilapidated old farmhouse on thirty-five acres of hardscrabble land with lake frontage on Bickford Pond.

Rev, fifty-something, a bona fide character, Boston socialite and musician, and Manny, highly intelligent, but physically and mentally war-damaged, were beginning their new life at "Journey's End" starting a tree farming business—something neither of them had any experience with, whatsoever.

Of the four main people involved in raising me, none of them had any experience with farming, beyond a backyard vegetable garden. There was no access to electricity in Porter, hence no running water and no plumbing. While Rev and Manny chose to live with kerosene lamps, water fetched from their dug well and a chemical toilet, my parents were ever so ready to welcome electricity when it was finally available.

While my parents shared basic values, the messages I received and perceived were sometimes conflicting. I soon learned which parent to ask for what. While Mummy was easier to convince, Daddy was more solicitous, advising me to find different solutions or to make do with what I had.

Growing up in Porter had its challenges, given that no one in my family was from Maine. Daddy had a gift for empathy and soon learned to fit in with the neighbors as well as with the business people in town. We had a lot to learn and thanks to the kindness of our neighbors, we did better than one might have expected.

Mummy had a harder time, but she found good friends over time. Her disdain for pretentiousness ostensibly kept her from joining social groups; I suspect she felt like a fish out of water. Coupled with her depression, the environment caused her to feel like an outsider for quite some time. This didn't change until she was befriended by a group of women in Parsonsfield ranging in age from their 30s to their 80s; they were irreverent and shared my mother's interest in books, liberal politics and the environment.

————

Through these stories, I have attempted to give glimpses

of how life was for me from my earliest memories until adolescence, when I acquiesced to my parents' wishes and went to Fryeburg Academy as a boarding student. My parents were relieved to have me in a safe environment where I could live on campus, expand my horizons and be active in after-school activities. In addition to in-state students, who came from communities without a high school, others came from across the United States and from foreign countries.

My stories are inspired by personal memories, from reminiscing with my sisters and poring over photographs and journals. The situations and feelings remembered and conveyed are true to my recollections. I include character sketches of family members, my godparents and colorful neighbors, while also sharing rich childhood experiences outside the classroom. Elementary school wasn't a good fit: I can recall having stomach aches and staying at home, in bed, being read to by Mummy and Rev. I don't wish to suggest that there weren't some good moments at school because there were, such as in fourth grade when an independent project studying honeybees engaged me in a way nothing previously had. But I was always happiest outside, exploring the world around me.

My childhood in rural Maine (less than a mile from the New Hampshire border) had a profound effect on the person I have become. I use the present tense because I continue to become—evermore slowly, from my aerie in Portland—where I look down on the harbor at the many activities and changes taking place, on and alongside the rising water level.

Our Porter neighbors lived lives guided by aphorisms and principles based on truths from life experiences. They were survivors who lived simply, some instilled with the fear of God. Others, out of necessity, were guided by the weather, closely observing cloud patterns and the behaviors of insects, birds and animals.

I feel privileged to have lived the life I lived at a time where children could be gone all day as long as they were home in time to wash hands in time to sit down for supper with their families.

Louise, Charlotte and Kathy, 1947

Charlotte Fullam

Swimming, 1948

Beginnings

Nardo and Alice, 1938

Family

From her bedroom window in Sherborn, Alice Davis caught a glimpse of a handsome young man helping his father prune fruit trees. She was so taken with Nardo that she showed up at the next Sherborn baseball game where he happened to be pitching. After the game Alice waited around, conspicuously, to speak with him. There was a mutual attraction.

Young people in Sherborn, Massachusetts got together on tennis courts, at Farm Pond and at baseball games; Alice and Nardo were no exception. They soon enjoyed tennis doubles matches, and it wasn't long before Nardo was invited to visit Maine for a long weekend with Alice and the Raffys. Nardo and Alice were smitten, and Katharine, romantic that she was, did her utmost to encourage their romance.

Bancroft, Alice's father, highly disapproved of the relationship and tried to buy Nardo off with a significant offer of money. But Nardo wouldn't be bought. Instead, he and Alice were married in a chapel in South Hampton, New Hampshire on September 16, 1940. Katharine and the officiating Episcopalian priest were the only attendees.

Following a honeymoon to New York City, Alice and Nardo moved to Kezar Falls, spending their first winter in an upstairs bedroom of the Raffy's renovated, but unheated farmhouse. That they endured this test of their relationship speaks volumes about the people they were.

I arrived just shy of a year later. Within five years, Alice and Nardo had three little girls: Kathy, Louise and me. Until just after Louise's arrival we lived in a five-room house with no electricity or plumbing. With increased exposure to laundry soap from washing clothes and diapers by hand, Mummy developed eczema on her hands, often leaving them raw and bloody. With Daddy and Rev's help Mummy made it through some difficult times, but with farm work to be done Daddy couldn't keep up. Gram Hadlock, in her mid seventies, deaf and savvy, was hired to live with us in what became known as Gram's room. Having raised at least five children of her own, she was just the person Mummy needed to help with everyday chores and child-rearing. She was a cherished part of our family.

––––––––

Mummy's love of horses, dating back to her childhood, had been an escape for her. She liked everything related to their care, from daily brushing, combing out manes, cleaning their hooves to cleaning tack with saddle soap. Before Louise was born Mummy had acquired Beauty, a dependable black mare who provided endless hours of riding and escape from housework and child care. An excellent rider, Mummy had few fears, even being unfazed by chance encounters with moose from time to time.

Alice and Nardo shared basic values when it came to child rearing, family and community life, even though they were from very different cultural, socio-economic and religious backgrounds. Daddy was more mercurial and extroverted; Mummy was introverted and frequently depressed, meaning that Daddy often juggled managing the farm, helping his wife and being there for us girls when she was depressed.

By the time I was seven, we were enjoying our own milk, butter, beef, and pork from a farm we owned across Bickford Pond, where a resident farmer, Frank Littlefield, tended our cattle and pigs with the devotion of a doting parent. His wife, Nettie, with an inclination to be a sourpuss, made delicious butter using a hand churn.

Daddy tried to enlist at the onset of WWII but he wasn't accepted because the Army wanted farmers to stay on their farms and raise potatoes and beans to help in the war effort. By the spring of 1943, instead of going off to war, Daddy plowed and disc-harrowed the flat, a large, level field at the edge of Kennard Hill Road. With help they planted six or seven acres of potatoes and beans which they harvested in the fall, keeping what they needed. The rest were sold to sustain U.S. troops.

Once the crops had been harvested, the same crew cut, dried and stacked firewood for use the following year, as kitchen wood stoves were used for cooking year-round, requiring firewood until the arrival of electricity in 1946. The wood stove served as a reliable source for heat and cooking, though the gas stove requiring electricity was a welcome backup.

The early success of the farm would not have been possible without the dedication and hard work of Frank Littlefield, Everett Eastman, and in later years, Ricky Libby. They had honed skills necessary to get the job done, and lived within two miles of us, which we considered the neighborhood.

In the 1940s farming required multiple skills: being able

to "read" or interpret signs from nature to predict the weather; keeping tractors, plows, disc harrows and mowing machines in good repair; knowing how to mow and rake hay into windrows; and knowing when it was dry enough to fork into hay wagons, then pitch the hay into hay lofts for winter use.

When machines failed, it was important to have the mechanical skills to know how to fix them. Farmers fared better with an understanding of crop rotation, companion planting and maintaining healthy soils in fields and forests without the use of commercial fertilizers.

Tree farming required understanding how trees thrive best, and in Daddy's case, pine trees in particular. He studied pests and understood that the pine plantation could be decimated in a single season (or two) if wild currant or gooseberry were found nearby. These invasives were immediately eradicated before blister rust could set in. In later years, monocultures, like the pine plantation, were proven to be as unhealthy for forests as for raising crops.

In addition to our daily rotating chores, there was always work to be done, but my sisters and I didn't mind, nor did we consider the work drudgery. We weeded, spread straw around tomato plants, picked hornworms off tomato plants and dropped them into jars of soapy water. We shelled dried beans and pulled mature onions to dry on open racks. Shelling peas was always fun. Mummy, and often Rev, sat in lawn chairs with bowls on their laps to catch the peas released as they popped open the pods and slid their thumbs between the halves. We girls sat on the grass shelling peas with our own bowl while Rev told stories of her childhood in Boston and time living abroad. Before tossing the discarded pods into the compost basket we sucked the juices from the fibrous pods until only strings of fiber remained.

In the summertime our family members could be found swimming, rowing and water skiing on Bickford Pond; picking wild strawberries, blueberries or blackberries in nearby pastures; picking beans and peas from the garden; hiking on nearby discontinued roads and fire breaks; horseback riding; and bird watching wherever we were.

Among my most favorite memories was going in late March as a family to the nearby patch of ground we called "the flat." At dusk we watched the mating ritual of male woodcocks on the open land, beginning with a series of nasal *peents*. Slowly the male flew upwards in wide circular spirals, twittering as he climbed. Once he was but a dot in the dusky sky, he suddenly plummeted to the ground, singing repetitively. His performance aimed to attract a female with whom to mate. He repeated the dance over and over, until it was too dark to be seen.

We enjoyed exploring back roads with the Jeep and having leisurely picnics in a pasture with a view. One of our favorite spots was just off the Cold Brook Road in Madison, New Hampshire—before or after black fly season. On a clear day this spot had a view that made Mt. Washington seem deceptively close, but it was actually 40 miles away!

On one of these picnics, I inadvertently slammed the car door shut on Kathy's hand while it was still in the hinge. Her shrieks brought Daddy racing back with the picnic basket still in hand. Daddy opened the door, extricated it and felt for broken bones before giving her hand a kiss, the medicine she needed as her sobbing turned to intermittent gasps as she recovered. Daddy picked her up and asked me to carry the basket as we made our way into the field to catch up with Louise and Gram Hadlock.

Winters were for tobogganing; skating on Bickford Pond and on the shallow duck pond; snow-shoeing across fields and on fire breaks; and sledding on the road to Colcord Pond.

On most days, only three or four cars passed by our house, including the mailman who drove slowly but faster than the other three. They crept by predictably, twice a day, on their way to and from Andy's store, just over the state line on Route 25, in Freedom.

Dad was delighted when conditions were right for pulling the toboggan behind the Jeep with two or three daring volunteers on board. Ideally, it had just snowed eight to ten inches, the road had just been plowed and the sand truck hadn't yet been by. Dad lashed the toboggan to the Jeep and drove up Kennard Hill at a steady clip with riders aboard. At the top of the hill the riders got off while Dad unhitched the toboggan, turned the Jeep around, re-lashed the toboggan, and, with riders again on board, drove back down the hill. This was even more tricky as the person in front had to stick their legs or arms out, fighting gravity, to keep the toboggan from sliding beneath the Jeep. Fumes from the exhaust added to the intoxicating ride! While we definitely found this exciting and fun, I was aware at the time that it wasn't a particularly smart thing to be doing.

On rare occasions when we were confined to being inside, we read and played cards. Old Maid was our favorite card game until we discovered bird rummy, butterfly rummy, and canasta. We also played checkers and Parcheesi until Scrabble took over in the early-mid 1950s. If stormy weather persisted we put on shows, handing out programs we had made for our audience, consisting of our parents, Gram Hadlock and anyone who happened to be visiting. Kathy and I did skits and a "Tea for Two" tap dance routine we'd learned at our dance lessons at the Hartford Pavilion. Our talent shows were varied, but Kathy could be relied on to play Schumann's "The Merry Farmer," while I recited poems and told jokes, and Louise performed "fancy" roping techniques.

In addition to learning new card games with Mummy, Gram Hadlock usually had ongoing projects for us in her bedroom where she kept her treadle-driven Singer sewing machine to mend clothes for our family when she wasn't hanging out the washing or cleaning the kitchen. That machine held a special fascination as it made sewing so much easier and faster. Gram patiently taught us how to use the sewing machine. Like most of our neighbors, Gram collected worn-out clothing, including ours; she never let anything go to waste. In addition to potholders, Gram taught us how to make latch hook rugs and embroidery samplers. Mummy taught us how to darn socks using a wooden egg; since there were always plenty of socks to be mended, that was a useful skill.

Among my favorite childhood memories was listening to Mummy read aloud to us at bedtime. She read books she had cherished: A.A. Milne's *Winnie the Pooh*, *When We Were Very Young*, and *Now We Are Six*; Kenneth Grahame's *The Wind in the Willows* and E.B.White's *Stuart Little*, which I read on my own but listened when she read it to my sisters. By the time White's *Charlotte's Web* was published, I had decided I was just too old to be read to, so I strained to listen from my bedroom as Mummy read to Kathy and Louise across the hallway.

Fortunately, I read *Charlotte's Web* on my own and was relieved that I didn't have to shed tears in front of my mother and sisters. *Charlotte's Web* brought tears every time.

Every month or two when we were having breakfast Daddy asked if any of us would like to go to visit his mother, our Nonna. Sometimes we all went, but Kathy could be counted as a resounding YES! She always wanted to go. Those day trips to visit Nonna in Sherborn, and later in Framingham, meant a delicious lunch awaited us. Knowing how much we loved her unsurpassable chicken cacciatore with polenta, Nonna always prepared it ahead, so that when we walked into her house the aroma filled the air. Nonna loved to feed us, and we loved being fed! Predictably, after we had finished lunch and had eaten a few dried apricots for dessert, with a twinkle in her eye, Nonna would say in her heavily accented, gravelly voice, "Now, you go home!" Daddy would reply with something that made her nod and smile before she repeated, this time with a higher pitch, "You go home! You go home NOW!"

It was time for us to go.

So we went.

Nardo

My paternal grandparents, Luigi and Annetta (Nonno and Nonna), were among the first Italian immigrant families to settle in Sherborn, Massachusetts, a small town eighteen miles west of Boston. Luigi, in addition to renovating a modest, two-story house on several acres of partially cleared land, with no formal training, painted accurately rendered foxes on their garage doors, an unusual sight in Sherborn. In some ways, their home felt like a visit to Taino, the small town in northern Italy where they both were raised. Missing were Lago Maggiore, azaleas, rhododendrons and salamis hanging to cure. Sherborn's Farm Pond was no Lago Maggiore, but it was a gathering place where townspeople swam and rowed boats in the summertime and played ice hockey and skated on its ice in the winter.

When Annetta wasn't cooking she planted flowers where a lawn would have been, scattering seeds at random, letting the seeds take hold where they landed, resulting in beautiful flowers where there had previously been a lawn. Along the driveway and throughout the landscape she planted hydrangeas, azaleas and rhododendrons to bring Taino ever closer, and Luigi tended to his own fruit trees when he wasn't tending those of his clients. Annetta also had a gift for handiwork, knitting wool socks, afghans and sweaters for her children, grandchildren and cousins.

Luigi and Annetta valued education, but in a way that made sense to them. Being Italian immigrants, they learned to speak English and developed skills that enhanced their quality of life in their newly adopted country. However, they remained proud of their Italian heritage and celebrated Italian customs they both cherished. A good example: Luigi and his sister Virginia singing arias from Italian operas after Annetta's scrumptious Sunday dinners with extended family.

Renato was born March 27, 1917, and his brother, Italo was born two years later. They were raised as Roman Catholic, yet Renato rejected his religion while still a young man. Since he never explained his rejection to his family, it remains a mystery.

Like all people, Renato was a composite of human qualities and emotions. He was loving, intelligent, athletic, passionate, mischievous, ill-tempered, a good listener, a champion of the underdog, musical, playful and moody. He could also be very funny. He adored children and they adored him in return.

Renato was not only photogenic, he had a big, winsome personality, an inquisitive mind, intelligence, a love of adventure and a love of people. It wasn't surprising that his family and neighborhood mentors became his support system, helping him gain traction as he took risks and explored his surroundings.

But there were hurtful moments along the way.

The first setback came in first grade when the teacher didn't like the sound of Renato's name and took it upon herself to rename him "Rinardo." The name stuck, along with Nardo, the name Alice gave him.

Nardo was passionate about music, especially music that evoked an intense emotional response. During his adolescence he became enthralled with jazz, and with New Orleans jazz in particular, loving its rhythms and improvisation.

Once bitten by the jazz bug he knew he wanted to play alto saxophone, and he wasn't about to let a lack of money stand in his way. He found a part-time job weeding strawberries at a farm within bicycling distance from home. Nardo had to be up and dressed by 4:30 a.m. to be at the farm by 5. For two hours he pulled dew-covered weeds in rows of strawberries before returning home, drenched, with just enough time to clean up and change his clothes for school. Weeding wasn't lucrative, but he was disciplined and encouraged by his father to work hard for whatever he wanted in life.

Still lacking enough money to buy a sax, Nardo took a job helping his dad with grounds maintenance for wealthy residents in Sherborn. Little did he know that one day his future wife would be watching him from her bedroom window.

Once he bought his sax, Nardo practiced tirelessly and learned to play by ear, listening to jazz greats: Louis Armstrong, Duke Ellington, Benny Goodman and vocalists Ella Fitzgerald and Lena Horne. He played along with them on 78 rpm records and on the radio.

At fifteen Nardo entered a musical competition at the Boston Opera House. He won first prize and was soon offered jobs in various clubs in and around Boston. However, his father worked long hours and couldn't take him to the clubs, and he wasn't about to let his son go without a trusted adult. Since there was no one to accompany him, Nonno encouraged his oldest son to keep up with his schoolwork instead.

Nardo loved those rare occasions when he could play with other musicians. As an adult he would sit in his favorite armchair, put on a record with Louis or Ella, close his eyes and raise his arms as if directing them, then sit on the piano bench, put the saxophone reed to his lips and slide into his own world.

Gifted in math, as many musicians are, when we asked for help with a math problem, his initial response was "Use your head! Never mind what the book tells you, what the teacher tells you. It has to make sense to you!" That was well and good for him, but what if it didn't make sense to us? He would solve the problem in his head while we struggled to work it out on paper.

Nardo was bullied, called a "wop" and denied a diploma at graduation because he allegedly didn't write well enough, despite excelling at math and passing all his classes. While that came as a painful shock after four years in high school, it didn't deter him. Where some would have accepted this as their fate, the assault on his integrity propelled Nardo to take his education into his own hands and seek out mentors who recognized and nurtured his abilities.

Following his senior year of high school Nardo applied for and got a job at Raytheon on an assembly line, manufacturing an electron tube that converted household alternating current to direct current for radios. He devised a system to automatically perform his part of the assembly so he could sleep long enough to go to a second more menial job, doing yard work. He managed to save enough money to buy his Pop a new Dodge sedan as well as a secondhand Dodge for himself and his soon-to-be bride.

Following his marriage to Alice, they relocated to Maine where Nardo eventually enrolled in correspondence courses in forestry at the University of Maine to learn how to best manage the pine tree plantation. He did plenty of physical work, and he also read multiple daily newspapers, journals on farming, forestry and finances. His financial acumen was the underpinning of his success. He became an informed investor in the stock market but never gave advice beyond "Know what's happening in the world. Stay informed. Even then, it's no more dependable than a horse race." He also did his own book-keeping, maintained records of milk production for each cow in the herd of 16, balanced financial books for logging and managed a crew of two, three or four workers.

Having experienced discrimination firsthand, Nardo instilled in us that people should not be judged by their personal attributes or circumstances. He remained consistent in this belief, demonstrating by his actions that it was unacceptable when anyone was judged on the basis of race, class, religion or sexual identity. While he had no tolerance for bullying, his own teasing could turn painfully close to bullying, and on occasion it crossed the line. To his credit, he usually apologized after reflecting on his volatile behavior.

Dad included photos and mementos from his grandchildren amongst his business papers. This brought smiles to his family and his accountant.

It wasn't unusual for him to have one or two of his daughters with him at the hay field or waiting endlessly as he made small talk while running errands in town. Kathy was his most constant companion, but I loved being with him at the Cornish Station as the train rumbled to a stop, its brakes hissing, before he boarded to pick up grain. On the way home Dad often stopped at the Kezar Falls National Bank, where I pleaded with him to not talk too long with Malcolm. On the way home, stopping at Carol Good's restaurant for her best-ever, homemade raspberry pie made waiting for Daddy much easier. Carol greeted me with a cheerful, "Zipperoo, how are you?"

Alice

My grandmother, Charlotte Davis, died when my mother and her brother Gerry were eight and ten, respectively. Though Charlotte was never a physical presence in our lives, she played an indirect, but important, role in the lives of my sisters and me. After Charlotte's death, our mother, Alice, suffered from depression that she never fully overcame, being the sensitive, intelligent woman she was. The loss of her loving, kind mother was heartbreaking. As Charlotte prepared for her death, she asked Katharine, her dear friend, to be a supportive presence in the lives of Alice and Gerry. Though neither of them had raised children, Katharine and Henri gave of themselves in every way they knew how.

They brought Alice and Gerry to their fixer-upper house in Porter, Maine where they spent winter vacations and long weekends with school friends. In addition to skiing, tobogganing and snowshoeing, Henri gave them French lessons, speaking only in French when they were vacationing in Maine. Those lessons must have worked because Alice spoke beautiful French, and Gerry probably did too.

Bancroft, Alice's father, was in his late sixties when Charlotte died. Alice recalled that on the day of her mother's death her father had breakfast as usual, and he didn't even acknowledge that their mother had died. Rather, he continued with his daily routine of having breakfast, reading the newspaper then going to the Boston Athenaeum, within easy walking distance.

While he physically lived at home with his children, he relied on others to attend to Alice and Gerry's basic needs. Bancroft had more of a relationship with Gerry, being a son and the eldest. Gerry was sent off to boarding school at Dexter, then to Milton Academy where he proved to be a most capable student. He followed in his father's footsteps to Harvard and then enlisted in the Navy where he trained French pilots, in French. He married Margaret "Peggy" Atkinson while still in uniform, and they lived on a naval base until the end of WWII. After the war Gerry went to Harvard Law School and graduated in 1947, the same year his first-born child, daughter Whitney, was born.

After the death of her mother, Alice continued on at Winsor School but her depression interfered with her studies. She resorted to drawing as an escape. Drawing became her refuge, revealing how truly gifted she was.

Alice may have inherited her tendency to depression from her mother, Charlotte. Happy memories at their summer house in Gloucester were short-lived, because looking out at the vast expanse of ocean caused Charlotte such sadness that the Gloucester house was sold, and another summer house bought in a rural setting, in Sherborn, Massachusetts.

Reading from Charlotte's teenage diary it's painfully clear that she did nothing spontaneously, that she forced herself to do everything but sleep. She scheduled multiple rest times throughout every day: after writing a letter, after taking a short stroll, after eating breakfast, after lunch and so on. Charlotte's younger sister, Minna, was not only very bright, but exceptionally beautiful and charming, no doubt adding to Charlotte's lack of self-esteem and depression.

————————

Alice and Gerry were raised Episcopalian, but neither was religious in any formal sense. Their upbringing was influenced by their parents and Katharine who all valued being well educated, well spoken and well read.

Alice loved nature and reveled in observing what was around her. She read voluminously and noted patterns in her observations, some of them disturbing like changes she saw happening in the natural world and to the climate. She was happiest on walks in the woods or on horseback, riding either alone or later with her daughters Louise and Kathy. She looked forward to the annual trail ride with Kathy and Louise and as many as fifty or sixty riders who came from all over Maine and New England to ride on discontinued roads during foliage season. Riders boarded their horses at the Cornish race track during the trail ride and convened for lunch in pastures with water troughs where riders could take a break and water their horses before letting them graze. Family members arrived with picnic lunches and, even for those of us who didn't ride, it was a social event that we looked forward to.

Prior to marrying Nardo, Alice had never boiled an egg. She dutifully learned to cook and soon prepared all the meals, actually becoming a very good cook, mastering the art of a "perfect" roast beef and Yorkshire pudding; producing loaves of crusty French bread; and making delicious fruit and berry pies. It's possible she may have regretted her accomplishments as they raised the bar for her family's expectations!

With the help of Gram Hadlock, our live-in housekeeper and surrogate grandmother, Alice learned how to can fresh vegetables with a pressure cooker that eventually blew its lid while she was canning green beans. I can still hear the hissing, growing louder and louder, until the lid blew off the pressure canner with a terrifying crash. When my curiosity got the better of me, I peered into the kitchen. My mother stood there, startled and shaken, "Dear, run out to the barn to see if Daddy's there. The pressure cooker just blew its lid!"

Katharine and Henri

Was it desperation? Loneliness? Curiosity? Or fond memories that prompted Henri Raffy to ask Katharine Foote to join him in Constantinople in 1923?

WWI officially ended in 1918, but the Ottoman Empire teetered on the verge of collapse for reasons still too complex for me to grasp. Henri had been promoted to First Lieutenant by the French Army, and I suspect he may have had a minor role in the "changing of the guard" in Constantinople. He had, after all, accepted the position of personal code officer for Louis Franchet d'Espèrey, Allied High Commissioner for the occupation of Constantinople. Henri was twice wounded at Verdun and more seriously at Les Butt es de Mesnil. He nearly died of malaria at Vardar, near Salonika. It was here he likely met d'Espèrey.

Katharine was volunteering as a Red Cross nurse at the French convalescent hospital in Tours. At some point he became her patient and conversations revealed shared interests in music, farming, languages, world affairs and people of all races, ages and ethnicities. When Katharine was reassigned to a hospital in England they continued their conversation—by mail. Their letter writing continued even when she returned home to Boston.

Without hesitation, upon receipt of Henri's invitation, Katharine set sail for Constantinople and they were reunited two weeks later. This was a man she knew mostly through correspondence. Interestingly, they both had nearly indecipherable handwriting. Henri's writing was precisely formed, requiring a magnifying glass to see the tiny letters in ruler-straight lines, while Katharine's carefree, loose script resembled unraveled yarn. How they managed to decipher each other's writing is a puzzlement!

They were married in an intimate chapel in Constantinople shortly after Katharine's arrival and moved to an apartment close to the bank where Henri worked. Katharine, meanwhile, wrote in her diary, which she later published in a small book: *Diary of a Red Cross Nurse*.

From the beginning they lived frugally, their one indulgence being a house-trained "watch-pig" who lived with them in their apartment. When people reacted to the pig with disgust, Katharine was quick to come to the pig's defense: "She was as smart and as clean as any dog we ever had. And smarter and cleaner than some humans!"

With the culmination of Henri's duties at the bank in Constantinople, they began their circuitous journey to the United States, sailing first to Martinique, the French-owned and French-speaking island in the Caribbean. It is unclear how long they were there, although it was probably five or six months.

When they left Martinique their destination was Boston, where Katharine's parents lived on Beacon Hill. Their stay in Boston was extended by the death of Charlotte Davis, Katharine's closest friend and my grandmother.

Katharine already had a relationship with Gerry and Alice and had promised Charlotte that she would be supportive of Alice after her mother's death. Katharine shared Alice's love of animals, especially horses and dogs. Katharine was known to speak with her dogs—even verbalizing what they'd said to her. She was a bit eccentric, but she definitely wasn't crazy!

————

Katharine and Henri knew they must find a way to make a living, while still honoring their commitment to Charlotte and her children. After several years of raising chickens in South Hampton, New Hampshire, they concluded that Henri was suffering from the physical demands of their small, commercial enterprise. One day an ad in *The Boston Globe* caught their attention: Farmhouse in need of renovation, 20 acres of land, bordering Bickford Pond in Kezar Falls, Maine.

After a drive from South Hampton, Henri and Katharine were ready to dedicate their energies to restore this remote homestead and make it their own. It became a favorite weekend retreat for Alice, Gerry and their friends.

————

Henri had a keen eye for architecture, and could see potential in the farmhouse. With his attention to detail and his ability to translate his vision to paper (to the nearest hundredth of an inch) he employed the skilled labor of local carpenters to realize his vision. They tore away at the building until it was back to its original hemlock frame, post and beam, attached with wooden pegs. This would become the home they both envisioned.

They were delighted with the restoration, though it had none of the amenities they'd become used to: electricity, running water and plumbing. It was also a six-mile walk to the nearest grocery store. And neither of them drove!

In addition to restoring the house and garage, Henri designed a barn influenced by those in the south of France. Built of oak and pine, and finished with linseed oil and turpentine, its steep roof was pitched to avoid snow buildup. The barn still draws attention with its contemporary lines and unusual yellow color.

Their descriptively named home, *Journey's End*, was a welcome respite for my mother Alice and her best friend Lil, as well as Gerry and his many friends. With no central heat the inside temperature must have hovered around freezing during the winter months. However, this old house offered an off-the-grid adventure in living simply: splitting and stacking wood, tobogganing, skiing, snowshoeing and, in the summertime, swimming, rowing and fishing on Bickford Pond. Evenings were spent in conversation, playing checkers and reading by kerosene lamps.

Henri and Katharine

The Littlefields

Dad hired Frank Littlefield and his wife Nettie to care for the small Guernsey herd at "the farm" on the other side of Bickford Pond in 1944. The farm, formerly known as the Eastman place, had been bought by Rev and Manny a few years before. It had a large barn across the road from the house with an attached garage and shop area.

Manny and Daddy had similar visions for the farm, seeing it as vital to a modest income. They sold milk to L.F.Stacey Farm in Kezar Falls, in addition to providing milk for our family, the Raffys and the Littlefields.

It turned out to be an ideal situation for Frank and Nettie when Daddy hired them: Frank as herdman and Nettie to be in charge of maintaining and cleaning the equipment used in milk production. In addition, she made butter from the cream for the Raffys, our family and for themselves. Frank and Nettie brought Eleanor, her adolescent daughter, and her ailing mother with them. The farm had three bedrooms, a big kitchen, living room and attached shed and workshop. The house was large and could easily accommodate a family of four.

Frank could be counted on to care for the cattle, which included milking them twice a day. He was dependable, experienced and knowledgeable. He was also an ideal herdsman, caring for the herd as though they were his well-loved children. He was gentle and kind with a sense of humor that could be missed if he didn't laugh himself—so hard that he emitted bursts of *hee-hee-hee*, repeatedly until his surrounding audience caught the giggling bug and everyone was laughing.

Frank had a special love for animals. Previously he had been responsible for caring for and driving teams of horses for logging operations in Maine's north woods, in the days before logging was mechanized. Winter temperatures were often sub-zero and living quarters were cramped and uncomfortable. Success of the logging operation depended largely on the cook who was responsible for providing enough calories for the loggers to work 10-12 hour shifts. Baked beans were a staple at every meal, in addition to oatmeal for breakfast and roast pork, biscuits or rolls and tea for supper, seven days a week.

Frank was a great resource. In addition to his gift for understanding animals, Frank played a concertina and had been a regular at dance halls in his younger days.

Nettie, anything but fun-loving, could be as sour as a gooseberry, but she churned delicious butter, was known for her donuts and made delicious pies—when the spirit moved her.

Eleanor, Nettie's daughter by a previous marriage, lived with Nettie and Frank until Nettie left Eleanor with Frank and returned to Cherryfield, her hometown. There she cared for her aging mother, and never saw her daughter again.

Several years later, Eleanor and Frank married and lived happily together for about fifty years.

Gram Hadlock

An addition to our house was in the process of being built prior to Louise's birth in 1946. At about that same time, electricity poles were being sunk into deep holes along the gravel road. Once the poles were secured in place, an electrician, with the help of a young assistant, strung the electrical wire along the poles.

Electricity and more living space were welcome additions, yet Mummy was visibly overwhelmed managing the household. She learned while speaking with her friend, Hazel, that Hazel's elderly mother, in her mid-seventies, was looking for housework and child care in exchange for a modest stipend and room and board. "Ma's as deaf as a post," Hazel explained, "but let me tell you: she knows how to work. Been at it since she was six!"

Ophelia Mae came to live with us a few days later. "Call me Gram. Everyone else does," she said with a warm smile. "I've raised lots of children, my own and other people's. There's never been a young one I can't get along with."

With Dad's help, Gram moved into the spare room downstairs. I was initially resistant to the idea of having a stranger move into our house but warmed slightly when Dad brought Gram's treadle-operated Singer sewing machine into her room. When I asked if I could watch her make potholders, she offered to show me how to make my own patchwork potholders. She was ever so patient with us and with her fifteen or so grandchildren.

Gram was with us on weekdays and on weekends when she wasn't staying with one of her children who lived close by. On rare occasions when we were left in Gram's care, one thing could be presumed: I would act out. One time I followed behind Gram as she climbed upstairs to say goodnight to each of us. Unbeknownst to her, I'd gone down the other set of stairs to follow up behind her. I could tell where she was by listening to her footsteps. She, on the other hand, relied solely on her eyesight—or so I thought.

By the time Grammy reached my room she was aware of my prank and sat at the end of my bed, waiting. Grammy had sensed the vibrations as I darted back upstairs, hiding behind doorways, waiting for her to notice that I was missing from my room. Sheepishly, I walked into my room. Grammy greeted me, "You must have been walking in your sleep!"

"Yeah, I don't remember getting out of bed. I wonder where I've been?"

Potato Harvest, 1943

Childhood

Charlotte Giovanella Fullam

Rev and Manny

My family used multiple names for those closest to us. Though not blood relatives, Katharine and Henri were the warp of the tapestry of my day-to-day life. Katharine, who featured prominently in my childhood, wore at least two identities for my sisters and me.

Mummy grew up calling her Aunt Katharine until her brother, Gerry, came up with the nickname Rev which he extracted from the French word for eighty: quatREVingt. Aunt Katharine was still in her sixties! The name *Rev* stuck like the fly paper in her kitchen and was used from then on.

Mummy always referred to Uncle Henri as Manny amongst our family and as Uncle Henri to everyone else. He was a more distant figure in my sister's lives but was, nevertheless, Manny to them as well. Next to Rev, I was the closest person to him. I first bonded with Manny in the vegetable garden as a three-year-old when I held brown paper collars for Manny to place around each tomato as he planted them in the scooped out earth. He took a shine to me, and I obviously enjoyed his attention as he read stories to me, including *Tintin*, in French. Afterwards, he explained the stories to me in English; I understood sometimes, but I loved the Tintin illustrations and made up my own stories based on those drawings.

Growing up in the 1940s offered a smorgasbord of

choices. Compared to many of my friends, I had a great deal of freedom, and with that freedom came responsibilities. Mummy posted our chores on a blackboard in the kitchen, and being the eldest I had more chores than my sisters. As soon as we were able we were responsible for making our own beds; folding and putting away our clean laundry; doing supper dishes; feeding the hens; cleaning out horse stalls; and feeding the horses their grain and hay. Neglecting our chores could result in forfeiting our allowance, something that rarely happened, since we liked doing chores.

The woods and fields were our playground, inviting us to build simple houses delineated with sticks. We'd watch the comings and goings of chipmunks or stir our stew pot, a natural hollow in a cluster of oak trees where water collected, to which we added grass, pine needles and dandelion leaves.

I collected birds' nests until Mummy discovered that my collection in the basement was alive with maggots; it was quickly disposed of. That left my feather collection of patterned and/or colorful bird feathers as my focus. On rare occasions I'd find a hawk feather lying on a path, and I'd feel as though the hawk had left a gift for my collection.

In late summer and early fall, small gray-black loon feathers, patterned with perfect round, white dots bobbed on the surface of the pond. From the rowboat I'd always scoop up a few for my collection.

I had options and I made choices, some choices were better than others, and I soon learned that with each decision came consequences. When I'd made an especially bad choice Dad would remind me, "You've made your own bed, and now you'll have to lie in it." This idiom was difficult for me to accept as a youngster.

———————

When the school bus stopped in front of my house at 4 p.m. to drop me off I secretly wished to run and play outside. Instead, I grabbed a quick snack and ran to the Raffy's where Manny would be waiting in his armchair, bathed in a haze of cigarette smoke; it was time for my French lesson. Together we reviewed nouns, pronouns, adjectives and adverbs; I conjugated verbs, repeating pronunciations until Manny gave his approval. *"Petit Chou, c'est bien fait, ça!"* That was my routine, five days a week.

Only in hindsight do I see how my life was shaped by my assumption that "my choice" to take French lessons wasn't my choice at all—but rather that I was fulfilling Rev and Manny's expectations for me. Though learning to speak and read French made me feel special, it also set me apart.

Yet, when given my druthers, I often chose to be with Rev and Manny rather than with friends. This may have been, in part, because I lived six miles from town, where the next house was a half mile away and vacant for most of my early school years, anyway. Early on I learned to find support wherever I could.

Rev and Manny were like a second set of parents. They adored me and I adored them, most of the time. I was aware of their bias and wished they weren't so critical of my sisters, especially Kathy, who took piano lessons from Rev and learned to read music well enough to accompany Dad on his saxophone. Though Kathy was a good pupil, Rev would easily become critical of her, once referring to her as a barbarian. A barbarian!

In later years Kathy said that being called a barbarian had actually given her strength to defend herself in other situations—that it made her stronger; had she not had a strong self-image, she might have suffered even more. I had wanted to jump to my sister's defense but had remained silent. I knew how unfair Rev was being, but I didn't have the courage to stand up for Kathy. Instead I chose to remain in Rev's good graces, avoiding her wrath at all costs.

————

Sometimes I simply enjoyed being in their home—where I was allowed to "carefully touch" the exotic treasures acquired on their travels in Europe, the Middle East, Southwest Asia, North Africa and Martinique.

I loved climbing the steep, winding stairs to the east bedroom where I could walk barefoot on felted goat hair rugs or pick up a rhythm instrument in the form of a long, brown pacay seed pod from Martinique whose seeds rattled when shaken. Just inside a large trunk was a celluloid flute with teeth marks where, as a younger child, I had chewed on the mouth piece. Beneath the flute lay an off-white, woolen burnoose from Algeria. Manny had acquired the massive, flowing, hooded cape while serving in WWI in the Maghreb in Northwest Africa, ruled at that time by the French.

Many of Rev and Manny's treasures were used daily. They weren't only practical, they added a dimension of interest, and even intrigue, to everyday chores. On a clear, dry day Rev might let me whack the rugs on the lawn with the rattan rug beater, bent into the shape of a Celtic knot. Or she might ask me to dust with her ostrich feather duster whose long handle made it possible to reach higher than I could see.

One of Manny's most prized possessions was a small Russian icon, a painting of three angels with gilded halos in cobalt blue and vermillion garments that hung beside the cluttered desk on the smoke-stained basswood paneling. An antique ceramic water pipe from the Middle East sat on the granite mantelpiece.

In the north room a smallish brass-framed clock with glass sides, through which I could watch its inner workings, stood on four, marble-size, brass spheres. Hundreds of books lined any wall space not taken up by windows.

As soon as you walked through the Raffy's front door you'd be greeted by the smell of cigarette and wood smoke, which hung in the air as a bluish haze, along with the the smell of kerosene from their lamps and the smell of Gambo, their old Newfoundland, and Banqui, an anxiety-ridden Pointer. I never became desensitized to the old dog smells, no matter how hard I tried.

Kathy and Louise

Katharine Anita was born at the end of July 1944. A week after my third birthday I was introduced to Kathy, a bundle swaddled in a cotton blanket with a small face protruding—not unlike the face of my doll, Patty Ann. Mummy and Daddy had tried to prepare me, but being just three, the idea of a sister was too abstract to grasp.

I watched with Rev from the back seat of our car as Mummy carried the baby and Daddy, by her side, carried the suitcase as they left the hospital. When they approached the car, Rev opened the back door to greet Mummy and her new namesake. Mummy handed the baby to Rev, who admired the precious baby she cradled her arms, cooing gently. I, on the other hand, wasn't so sure about this baby. Mummy hadn't seemed to notice that I was sitting beside Rev, and now they were both admiring a baby.

What about me?

On the trip home Rev held the baby and helped me feel included by pointing out that the baby had no eyebrows and no fingernails. *Why? Is something wrong?* Actually, nothing was wrong. Since Mummy had to have C-sections the doctor wanted the baby to be on the smaller side. Kathy was quickly gaining in size, so the doctor had made the decision to deliver her early.

My first encounter with Kathy made an indelible

impression. She lay in Rev's arms sleeping peacefully as Rev pulled the blanket away from her little hand and asked if I'd like to hold it. *With no fingernails?!* It was a strange sensation, feeling her tiny hand in mine. I bit my lower lip, intrigued but aware that already my sister was garnering attention—attention that might otherwise have come my way.

Kathy was an effervescent, fearless toddler who delighted her family with her wide smile and happy-go-lucky nature; she would soon become Daddy's sidekick. At some point, while still under a year old, she stood in her crib and brought down the moveable side. She wanted out! Kathy walked almost as soon as she could stand, and by the time she was four I knew that she was stiff competition. She was strong and at least as determined as I was.

On more than one occasion we stood at the top of the stairway pulling each other's hair until one of us gave in!

—————

One morning as we ate breakfast, Kathy and I were surprised to see a dark green, canvas tent at the edge of the field. Daddy had set it up earlier that morning to surprise us. We ran, barefoot, through the wet grass, to have a closer look.

"Let's go in," I suggested. "You go," Kathy urged with hesitation. She wasn't going to step inside until she could be assured that there were no bats lurking in the dark corners. Peering inside, the tent was dark, dank and smelled of moldy canvas. Now, I wasn't so sure I wanted to step in either. We stood by the tent flap, intrigued yet hesitant.

"I'll go in, but you have to come in right behind me," I coaxed. "No one can find us," Kathy said as she entered. I looked around, keeping my eye on the entrance, "We need a blanket. Let's ask Mummy if she has one."

We ran back to the house, and Mummy gave us the brown wool, fringed picnic blanket. She offered to help spread it out in the tent, but I assured her, "Kathy and I can do it." Once we'd spread the blanket, making a sort of floor, we moved our dolls, blue willow dishes and a doll's high chair onto the blanket. "Now there's no room for us! Let's move everything off the blanket so we can have room to sit down," I suggested.

The tent was our go-to place—until we saw a spider, a *large* spider on the tent wall. We each had our dislikes: I was fascinated by snakes as long as they didn't touch me; Kathy was terrorized by bats and butterflies; and Mummy was afraid of spiders. Even though spiders weren't a phobia for either of us, the spider on the tent wall gave us both the willies! It was easily the size of the palm of my child-size hand.

It wasn't long after we saw the spider that Daddy took down the tent to mow the field. With Mummy's help we spread the blanket on a spot beneath the elm tree, where we played until Kathy's morning nap. Looking back, it interests me how making a house required only boundaries, such as a blanket.

After our busy day Mummy called us to come in for supper. "We have some news for you," she said. "Come wash your hands before we eat."

"How would you like to have your own bedrooms?" Daddy asked.

"I would," I said. Kathy, only two and a half, was busily eating.

"That's good, because we have to make room for a baby

who will be arriving in late May."

Daddy added, "Manny is helping us design an addition for our house that will suit our need for more space and fit within our budget."

I wrinkled my face, clearly not understanding what Daddy was saying.

Daddy tried to simplify his explanation, "Honey, it's setting aside the money we have to build the addition and not spending more than that."

Still not understanding what a budget was, I moved on. "Where will the baby sleep?"

Mummy answered, "In the room you and Kathy now share."

"Maybe the baby will hear Santa's reindeer on the roof the way we did!"

—————

The builders arrived on the first day with an excavator to dig the foundation. I wanted to watch from outside, but Mummy said I should watch through the window so that I wouldn't get in the way. Kathy stood by me at the window as the excavator dug into the ground, lifting buckets of dirt onto a truck. Two of the men marked the corners with posts. The next day they set up forms for the basement walls, and once the forms were in place they poured concrete into the forms. It took the concrete over a month to cure so the builders worked on another project before returning to frame the addition. That was followed by putting up walls, attaching lath and then plastering over the lath.

The best part of the building process came when Bob MacDonald built and installed a storage closet and cabinetry in the kitchen. Our family adored him and Daddy came up with Macky Doodle as a name of endearment for Bob's warmth, kindness and playfulness. He clearly liked and understood children, entertaining us with whimsical stories. He even made wooden jewelry boxes, in the form of chests of drawers, for each of us. When Bob and his wife, Hazel, stopped in while out for a Sunday drive, we were in for a treat. They were tickled by everyday happenings and by each other.

When the ell was completed, Kathy and I moved into our new bedrooms. The addition also had a playroom, winterized porch, basement and vestibule on the old part of the house.

Mary Louise arrived at the end of May 1946 and was called Louise from the very beginning. Mummy soon found in her a kindred spirit, a lover of horses—a bright, quiet, gentle soul. Daddy often read to her while she was a toddler, usually the same story, *Spunky the Pony*. After a full day's work, he would be almost asleep on the bed beside her, attempting to skip a word or two to stay awake. Louise would correct him every time, having memorized the entire story.

Louise displayed a love for and connection with horses from her first encounter with Beauty while still in Mummy's arms. As soon as she could walk, she wandered out to the pasture where she clung to Beauty's leg as the horse grazed. While neither of our parents seemed too worried about us when we played outside, Mummy must have had some concern about Louise's safety, because after seeing her wrapped around Beauty's leg, she put a child's harness on Louise and tied her to whatever seemed stable and out of harm's way. In spite of being tethered, Louise and Kathy played happily in the sandpile, by the bulkhead or under the elm tree with their dolls.

Being older than Kathy and Louise, I preferred to be on my own, making houses in the woods and collecting birds' nests and feathers, seed pods and rocks. Every now and then I was tempted to play with them because they were having such a good time, but as soon as I approached everything would change. Mummy often reminded me that "two's company; three's a crowd." She was usually right.

And so it was with us most of the time, except on Christmas Day. That was a time when we had fun as sisters, rising before dawn and tiptoeing downstairs to see if Santa had eaten the cookie and drunk the glass of milk we set out for him after hanging our stockings by the fireplace on Christmas Eve. We carried our stockings to my bedroom where we emptied them to get to the treasured tangerines. There was something special about peeling our tangerines and eating the juicy little sections so early.

After we each unwrapped one more stocking gift, we went back to bed and slept until the smell of bacon wafted upstairs. Christmas breakfast was always a treat: fresh grapefruit, bacon, toast, scrambled eggs and milk or cocoa. Before opening presents we cleaned off the table, did the dishes and went to the playroom where Daddy would be listening to Bing Crosby sing "White Christmas."

Making Do

Whether it was feathers to adorn a headdress or yarn and knitting needles, Mummy invariably suggested that I go outside where opportunities for discovery were boundless; she was surely hoping my attention would be redirected elsewhere. But in fairness to Mummy, if my initial needs hadn't been forgotten, she did what she could to help me find whatever I thought I needed. I can't recall ever being deprived or wanting for much of anything, except a set of day-of-the-week underpants, a different color for each day.

Possessions didn't play a prominent role in my family. But being outside, playing in and observing nature did. "Pay attention," was Dad's advice at least once a day, implying that we must always pay attention, no matter what we were doing.

Unless the weather was stormy, Mummy saw to it that my sisters and I went outside to "get the good of the day." As soon as we were able to walk confidently alone, we were free to roam in the horse pasture, "the little woods," and to the pine plantation across the road, on a steep hillside that rose to "the cathedral," where a mixed forest of stately trees stood high above Colcord Pond.

Among my earliest memories are of making gloves, putting the soft bell-shaped petals of foxglove blossoms on my fingertips; picking buttercup blossoms to hold beneath my sisters' chins to see if they liked butter and making daisy chain crowns to wear in my hair.

At age seven I was inspired by a newspaper photo of paratroopers jumping from a plane into battle. I certainly had no allusions of going into combat, but that photo gave me, what seemed then, a very good idea. Having a shape much like a parachute, an umbrella would also trap air, or so I thought. I stood at the edge of the hayloft holding Daddy's fully opened black umbrella with my arms outstretched above my head. I looked down the ten feet and jumped. The umbrella inverted immediately, and I crash landed onto scatterings of hay below.

Since I had failed with the umbrella, I thought I might have better success making and flying a kite. Mummy had given me a *Do It Yourself* craft book for Christmas, and in it were directions for making a kite. We had all the necessary materials, including scissors, ruler, paper punch, a brown paper bag (instead of butcher paper, which we didn't have), a ball of string, and Scotch tape.

I followed the directions meticulously, first cutting off the plain side of the bag, folding the paper in half, then measuring points on the folded paper with the ruler and connecting the points, just as the instructions indicated.

When I cut out the lopsided diamond shape, it looked just as it was supposed to. All was going well. However, since Mummy didn't have a wooden skewer to stabilize the kite, I had to go outside to find a long, thin stick to tape across the top of the kite's diamond shape, corner to corner. Next, as instructed, I punched a hole at the center of the bottom, on the fold line, about ¾ inch from the edge, then cut off two pieces of Scotch tape to put over the hole, one on the front and one on the back. I lined up the puncher over the taped holes and punched again to remove the tape from the holes. Then I attached the tail, about six feet of string, to which I tied four-inch by one-inch pieces of newspaper, twisted in the middle and looking like bows of ribbon (except they weren't as colorful). I tied them in the center with more string and attached them to the tail until there were ten in all.

It was ready to fly, and so was I! I took it out to the horse pasture with the tail inching closer to the ground with each step. "Stay far away from any light lines," Mummy warned as she hung out a load of washing.

There was only a breeze, nothing close to the wind I needed, but that wasn't deterring me. I held the kite from the cross stick and ran with it, the tail flopping behind. This procedure was getting me nowhere. After endless attempts to get my kite airborne I gathered up the kite with its tail and went back to the house. When Mummy came in she said, "I think you'll need to wait for a windier day."

When that day arrived, I still had high hopes that I'd watch my kite soar above the treetops. The elms were especially tall, and I wasn't sure I had enough string for my kite to fly that high, but I wanted, above all, for my kite to be airborne. So back to the pasture I went. The wind was blowing so hard I thought it might rip the kite while I was still holding it. Taking the kite by its cross piece in one hand and the ball of string in the other, I ran, letting go as the wind caught my kite. It flew up about five feet and tumbled back to the ground. The attempts continued, but for the sake of my readers, let me say that I never did get that kite to fly.

In that same pasture was a stand of oak trees, including

a clump of four oaks whose bases were joined together two feet above ground level, forming a deep indentation that my sisters and I quickly recognized as a perfect "stew pot." We spent countless hours stirring the pot with a stick, admiring the "stew," adding acorns, lamb's quarters, grass and pine needles to the mixture of rotted wood and rain water until the mixture was suitable to feed to our favorite stuffed animals and dolls. No taste tests needed!

Dad gave me access to wood scraps from which I eventually built a house, nailing one side to one of the oaks where we had our stew pot. What I remember best about that house is that I got Mummy to sit in it with me during a rainstorm to show her that the roof didn't leak. I quickly learned that the entrance needed a barrier because the wind-driven rain soaked us both, sending us both dashing across the field and into the house to change into dry clothing.

My "experiments" followed a familiar pattern, but I never let this deter me from further experimentation. This pattern of making do and doggedly staying the course has remained consistent throughout my life.

Miss Aubrey

TommyWhiskers lay contentedly on the braided rug beside my rocking chair. Long, twitchy ripples ran down Tommy's back as I stroked his soft fur. The aluminum kettle whistled wildly, sending water droplets skittering across the cast-iron stovetop. Mummy was upstairs, changing the beds; Daddy was working in the barn. I was waiting for Miss Aubrey.

The sun glanced off the granite steps—a sure sign Miss Aubrey would soon appear. Eager to see my friend, I went to the front door, stood on my tiptoes and tried to open the latch just out of reach. Mummy heard me fumbling with the door, because the next thing I knew, she was next to me, holding my jacket.

"I can see you're anxious to get outside," she said.

Mummy helped me with my jacket, one arm at a time. Then boots. I held her shoulder as I stuck out one leg, then the other, while she tugged my boots on, over my shoes. Finally ready, she opened the front door and noted: "Spring is in the air!"

I stepped down, one step at a time, to a patch of bare ground bathed in sunlight. Snowbanks that surrounded the now exposed ground were once taller than I was. As they melted, snow fleas silently moved along them in droves, like tiny stitches of black thread.

Bright green daffodil shoots poked through the lingering snow along the granite foundation. Miss Aubrey was nowhere to be seen. I squatted beside my cooking tools: a wooden spoon, a tin cookie cutter and a baking sheet. The dirt was soft and moist as I scooped spoonfuls into the cookie cutter and onto the baking sheet. Miss Aubrey loved my mud cakes!

Blue jays screeched as they circled above the maples, clearly agitated. There was movement on a lower branch, but I saw nothing out of the ordinary until a speck of dazzling pink caught my attention. It was the same tulip pink as Miss Aubrey's dress. I stared at the splash of color as it moved along the branch, coming my way.

"Miss Aubrey!"

She waved and looked as she always did in her pink dress with ruffles, her pearl earrings and her dark brown hair rolled under, along the nape of her neck. She was Mummy's age, but ever so much smaller. Stuart Little's trousers would have fit her but Stuart Little hadn't been born yet. Besides, Miss Aubrey would never have worn trousers. We talked as a blue jay landed on the branch beside her. It cocked its head in her direction, screeched loudly again, straightened its legs, then raised its wings and flew away, with Miss Aubrey clinging to the jay's spidery legs! I watched in disbelief as they faded from sight.

I never saw her again.

———

Sixteen years later, when assigned my student teaching semester at The Park School in Brookline, Massachusetts, my supervising teacher was none other than Miss Aubrey. She had grown... considerably!

Packages for France

It was a typical day in late March: blustery and cool. WWI had ended, and while far too young to understand politics, I was aware that Manny spent hours every day, listening to war commentary, usually Cecil Brown or Edward R. Murrow. At such times Manny was not to be interrupted—for anything more minor than a house fire!

Rev could be rather clumsy and unerringly distracted Manny's ability to listen to the broadcast. As a twice-wounded war veteran it didn't take much to trigger a *crises de nerfs.*

With no central heat, a small, cast-iron cookstove in the kitchen and a fireplace in the living room, Rev and Manny retreated to those two rooms and an adjoining bedroom during the winter months. I have vivid memories of their cluttered, smoke-filled living space. In addition to small logs smoldering in the fireplace, Manny chain-smoked unfiltered Chesterfields that emitted a bluish haze that hung in the air until spring, when it was finally warm enough to open the windows. After he suffered a cerebral hemorrhage, Manny's friend and physician, Dr. Magnus Ridlon instructed him to smoke no more than one cigarette per hour, per day. Taking the doctor at his word, Manny set his alarm on the hour, every hour of every day—twenty four hours a day!

———————

By the first of March sunlight poured through south and west-facing windows, warming the summer kitchen that had been closed off during winter months to retain heat in their "inner sanctum," Rev's term for their winter living space.

Throughout the darkest winter months Manny, never one to be idle, gathered supplies for his French compatriots who, after the German occupation, still suffered from a shortage of basic supplies. With the precision of an engineer, he meticulously converted the dining table to a workstation where he, with Rev's help, packed cardboard boxes with medical supplies, shoes, clothing and non-perishable foodstuffs. Sending care packages was his obsession, his *raison d'être*.

I observed the exacting process from a nearby chair. Each box was wrapped with brown wrapping paper then taped shut at the seams. Rev measured sisal twine with a yardstick and cut it to fit around the box, leaving enough extra to tie knots. Lots of knots. Manny first created a box secured like a birthday present, wrapping vertically, beginning at the center and working out on either side, repeating the process horizontally. He secured a knot at each intersection until the entire box was covered in exacting rectangles of sisal twine, delineated by knots.

As a four-year-old onlooker, I was at once fascinated by the process and distressed by the anxiety Manny created for Rev. She was not inclined to precision, even when playing the piano. She would sweep her hands over the keys, hitting enough notes to show her audience that she was an accomplished player. Even her handwriting appeared as a scrawling, wavy trail of green ink, with vague symbols scattered along the path.

Creating packages knotted like tight macramé didn't reflect who Rev was. Manny's harsh reprimands of her awkward attempts to help were hurtful and had only negative effects on the production of packages for France—a noble cause, but with a human cost.

As I reflect on those tension-wrought sessions, it's clear that Rev had needed a break from a husband whose post traumatic stress disorder and obsessive compulsive disorder were exacerbated by living cheek by jowl in two rooms of their house during the long winter. Why she agreed to it is another puzzlement. It's also entirely understandable why Rev planned a long weekend in Québec City after the packages had been delivered to the Kezar Falls Post Office. She needed a break, and Manny surely welcomed the solitude.

First Train Trip

Two weeks later Mummy drove us to Union Station in Portland, an hour and twenty minute drive from Porter. From the backseat I watched the landscape change from trees to fields, to towns, more woods, more fields and new housing developments. Beyond the Westbrook brickyard, Mummy pointed out that we were in the city and just minutes away from the station.

As we turned into the parking lot, Union Station was a destination unto itself. Mummy parked the car near the station entrance. It looked like a castle with its tower and cone-shaped turrets. I was agog, taking in everything as Mummy, with my hand firmly in hers, coaxed me along, reminding me that Rev and I had a train to catch.

Rev waited by the entrance as we hurried to catch up. A porter wearing a beige uniform with dark red trim and a cap with a shiny black visor greeted us. He approached Rev, glancing sideways at our bags as he walked toward us. Rev handed him a tip, which he put in his pocket while asking where we were going. "I'm taking my godchild to Québec City," Rev explained.

Rev and I moved to the front of the forming line while the porter put tags on our bags. She stood behind me until the conductor called out "A-w-w-l - a-b-o-ah-d—train to Que-WEE-bec Cit-TEE," dragging out the words in a sing-song voice. I checked to make sure Mummy was still behind us before we boarded. The conductor held out his hand as I reached for the step with one leg while standing on the other, trying not to fall backwards. Rev remained right behind me. Once on the platform I looked one more time to make sure Mummy was still there. I waved to her with Rev nudging me along as my mother snapped pictures with her Brownie camera. The train hissed, sending steam out from beneath its engine, then hissed again with the fierceness of a monster.

We no sooner settled into plush velvet seats when Rev suggested we sit where we could wave to Mummy. I stood at the window to get a better look and waved again before the train left the station.

The conductor closed the door and made his way through the coach, speaking with passengers along the way. "May I see your tickets?" he asked Rev. She brought her handbag to her lap and reached inside for the tickets; she handed them to the conductor who punched both then handed them back. He winked at me as he moved to the next passenger.

Slowly the train moved onto the main track, then picked up speed, swaying and jerking to my utter delight. Rev stood reaching for my bag in the overhead compartment when the train gave a wrenching jerk that almost made her lose her balance. She passed me a book from my bag, which I put down on the seat beside me. I had my eye on the shiny water dispenser that I'd seen as soon as we entered the coach car.

I stood up with one hand on Rev's knee, "I'm thirsty!" Rev nodded wearily as I stood and stepped into the aisle. I walked by passengers of all ages, noting that I seemed to be the only child aboard. When I got to the water dispenser I was instantly drawn to the cone-shaped paper cups. They could actually hold water! And they were just the right size for my hand!

Reaching up, I placed my hand around the paper cone and pulled until the cup released. As I placed it under the water spigot, I turned the handle to release the water. This was tricky. Water streamed from the spout and quickly filled my cup to the brim. In the nick of time I turned the handle back to stop the flow of water, but in so doing I squeezed my cup too hard. Water spilled onto my arm and shoes. Not knowing what to do, I lifted the cup and drank what remained then filled my wrinkled cup once more. I returned to my seat and sat down beside Rev, waterlogged.

Rev was immersed in her book and raised her brow, but kept reading as I sat down. I didn't feel too well. Then I lowered my head, knowing I couldn't escape the inevitable: I was about to be sick...

"Uh-oh! I need to go to the bathroom! Right now!" I blurted.

Rev dropped her book on my seat and stood up; but it was too late. I threw up in the aisle while Rev held my head and kept my braids away from my face. I was unsteady as she held my hand, guiding me toward the bathroom. Rev opened the narrow door and peered inside. "I'm not sure we can both fit, but we'll try!" she said. We tried and we succeeded—long enough for her to moisten a hand towel in the little brass sink that she used to wash my face and hands. With another damp towel she cleaned my clothes and the ends of my pigtails. "There, there. You'll be fine," she assured, but I wasn't convinced. I wanted to go home.

Once I was cleaned up we headed back to our seats. Rev

noticed that someone had kindly cleaned up the aisle. We sat back down and I curled up with my head in Rev's lap. I fell into a deep sleep and didn't wake up until Rev gave me a gentle shake as we approached Québec City.

With help from the conductor we got our bags from the overhead compartment and prepared to exit. I was trying to be as brave as Rev so often reminded me I was; but I still didn't feel well.

I was half asleep when we left the coach, because we had somehow made it to the sidewalk in front of the train station where Rev hailed a taxi.

"*Où allez-vous?*"

"*À l'Hotel Clarendon, s'il vous plait!*"

Waves of nausea continued to pass over me as we drove through the city. Within minutes that felt like hours, the driver pulled up in front of our hotel. The concierge sent our bags to our room and handed Rev our room key. We walked up to the second floor, and Rev just opened the door to our room when I made a beeline for the bathroom—just in time this time!

Rev suggested I take a warm bath, which sounded good to me. She put the rubber plug in the drain and opened the faucets, placing her hand into the running water to be sure the temperature was neither too hot nor too cold. I undressed, stepped into the warm water and slid down until only my face was above the warm water. While I soaked, Rev called the front desk and ordered an extra towel and a sponge.

Our room overlooked a lawn with beds of daffodils and tulips. Ordinarily, I would have wanted to run around on the lawn. Instead, after drying off and slipping into my nightgown, I lay down on the cot the concierge had set up.

I was almost asleep when Rev called the front desk for room service. The thought of dinner made me feel sick all over again.

I tried not to look when Revy's meal was delivered. I tried even harder not to smell it. Rev ordered a small bowl of beef consommé for me, but I couldn't even look at it. I went back to the bathroom, stared into the bowl of water and thought I would throw up again. Instead, I brushed my teeth, washed my hands and face, and went back to bed while Rev sat, poised on the edge of her bed with her tray, eating her supper.

"Dors bien, petit chou," she said, wishing me a good night's sleep.

"I'd like some ginger ale," I said feebly.

Rev answered, "I'm sure we can get some."

A knock on the door awakened me, and when I turned over in bed a woman with a gray dress and blue apron was handing Rev a glass of ginger ale. Rev thanked her and closed the door, stepping over to my bedside. "Drink just a few sips to see how that settles," Rev advised. I took a few sips and wanted more. "You see? You're on the mend!" Rev announced, cheerfully.

I went back to sleep and Rev sat reading in an armchair beside her bed.

The next morning when I woke up Rev wasn't in the room. She had eaten breakfast in the hotel café while I slept. When she returned I was still in bed, wondering where she might have gone.

"Dearest, I'm going to go out for a while. I brought you some more ginger ale. If that stays down I'll get some toast for you when I get back. Meanwhile, stay in bed and rest. If you need anything, someone at the front desk can help you. Just pick up the phone and say, 'front desk.'"

Rev assured me she wouldn't be gone long as she kissed the top of my head. As soon as the door shut behind her I brought my bag of books to the cot, but I didn't feel like reading. I tried to be brave and not to think about where Rev was. I just wanted to be home.

I must have fallen asleep, because when I awoke, I heard children's voices on the patch of lawn below my window. *I'm feeling so much better.* I opened my suitcase and picked out my clothes for the day. I dressed, put on my shoes and a coat. I was going out to play too!

The back stairway, next to our room, was steep. As quietly as a four-year-old could, I went down the stairs, one step at a time, holding onto the railing until I came to a back door in a hallway.

From the doorway I watched a girl and boy running around, chasing one another. The girl was older than I was, but when she noticed me standing there, she came over to "inspect," then with a swoop of her arm, she beckoned me to join in. They spoke French, and while I didn't understand what they said, it didn't really matter. They were having a good time, and I wanted to be a part of it.

Within seconds the girl's brother tagged me as he ran past. Before I had a chance to tag someone else, their mother came to the back door and called to them. *"Mes enfants, nous devrons partir!"*

They had to leave. With cursory waves they ran to their mother. Alone again, not knowing what else to do, I headed back to our room, upstairs. A lady with a gray dress and blue apron was making our beds, so I waited alone in the hallway.

After what seemed like a very long wait, I heard Rev's

voice coming from downstairs. *"À plus tard, Madame!"* Rev's deliberate footsteps coming up the stairs was both exciting and scary. When she noticed me standing in the hallway she asked why I wasn't in our room. I explained that there was a lady in a gray dress making our beds and I was waiting for her to finish.

Unable to contain my excitement I told Rev that I'd gone outside and played tag with a boy and a girl. Rev wasn't as surprised as I expected. She said, matter of factly, that I must be feeling much better. "Yeah, I am!" I replied.

The maid gathered her cleaning supplies and was on her way to the next room when Rev thanked her.

"You must be hungry by now! Are you ready for some lunch?" Rev asked.

"Yeah, I am. I'm feeling pretty hungry," I said.

"Then, let's wash our hands and go down to the hotel café."

"Okay! I'll wash my hands first," I said, going into the bathroom.

When I came out to dry my hands, Rev went into the bathroom and closed the door, coming out a little later. "Shall we go down to the café?" she asked.

"I'm ready, Revy."

We walked through the hallway to the main staircase, going down to the ground level. I followed Rev into the café where she was greeted warmly, having had her breakfast there earlier. Rev chose a table by a window. It was too high and out of my reach, so Rev asked for a bolster. The maitre d' returned with the pillow that was just right. He suggested that we try their carrot soup. "I'd like a grilled cheese sandwich!" Rev agreed that that was a good choice after having been sick. When the waiter came to our table, Rev placed two orders of carrot soup and said we'd share a grilled cheese sandwich.

————

After lunch Rev followed me up the stairs to our room. She said she thought I'd like what she had planned after we'd each taken a short nap. She removed her low-heeled strap shoes and curled up on her side on top of her bed with one arm tucked beneath her head. She was soon asleep. I watched from the easy chair as she drew in deep breaths, filled her cheeks with air, then blew out the air with an audible *puh*. She repeated this over and over. I took off my shoes and lay on my cot looking at books until I, too, fell asleep.

Rev was reading at the desk when I woke up. She looked up and smiled. She asked if I was ready for an adventure. I didn't know what she had in mind, so I didn't know if I was ready or not! She explained that we'd need to be dressed to go outside—which meant putting on our shoes and warm coats, to be ready for whatever came next.

The wide steps leading from the hotel down to the street were tall and steep. I followed behind Rev, hanging onto the railing to get to the sidewalk below. A carriage with wooden wheels, drawn by a tall white horse with a dappled gray rump, was waiting for passengers on the Rue Ste. Anne.

Rev asked me if I would like to take a ride. She said that the driver would take us to both sections of Old Québec: the upper city—where we were staying—and to the lower city that was along the St. Lawrence River. She looked directly at me, her eyebrows raised, as though pleading with me to agree. I wasn't at all sure that I wanted to take the carriage ride. I also wondered if the horse would stop moving long enough for us to get into the carriage. I felt small and timid.

Rev lifted me into the carriage where I sat on the seat looking backward because the driver blocked my view looking forward. The horse stepped sideways again, and the driver waited as Rev settled into the seat across from me. The driver glanced back to be sure we were ready to begin our adventure. *"Allons-y!"* he said, clicking his tongue and gently tapping the reins on the horse's back. We were on our way, heading toward the heart of the Haute-Ville.

I liked the sound the horse's hooves made as we rode along cobblestone streets, passing little shops decorated with red and white flags with red maple leaves. This turned out to be a good surprise adventure after all!

We stopped at a little square with stone buildings and a stone church. The driver explained that the explorer Champlain had once been in this very place. By this time, though, I wondered when we'd go back to the hotel. Our horse walked with his head bent down. Rev said he'd made this trip so many times before, he might be walking in his sleep!

We'd been in the carriage for more than an hour when the driver told Rev that he would be picking up more people at the famous Hotel Frontenac.

The Hotel Clarendon was just ahead; we'd be getting off there. At last! We thanked the driver, and Rev paid him as we left the carriage. *"Merci monsieur!"* I said, pleased that I dared speak two words of French.

"Bonne visite au Québec!" the driver said, clicking to his horse as he lifted the reins, tapped them again gently along the horse's back and pulled away from the curb.

Return From Québec City

Hattie Sargent

After WWII, our neighbors, Hattie and Ernest Sargent, contracted with a canning factory to harvest blueberries on a hillside across the road from their farm. There was already an abundance of wild blueberries on the rocky terrain that had belonged to Ernest's family for more than a few generations, but it was Hattie's entrepreneurial vision that saw the potential. Once she had the idea, she was motivated and nothing would stop her.

The company sent a field worker who burned the hillside every other fall or spring if it was a dry fall, because the ground needed to be damp. Burning kept the bushes from becoming overgrown and the resulting potash nourished the blueberries. Having a few patches of snow on the ground was ideal in case the wind picked up while they were burning, the snow would act as a barrier to contain the fire.

From my bedroom window across the pond I watched as an orange glow spread over the hillside. The desperate cries of the loons signaled danger on the pond. *Did the fire drive a predator to the cove where the loons were nesting?* Concerned, I rolled over and checked to see if, the fire had gotten out of control. All appeared quiet on the blueberry land.

In mid-June, once the berries had set on, the company

field worker returned with a large tank of insecticide mounted on the rear of his Ford Ferguson tractor. He sprayed the blueberry fields with chemicals that would prove devastating in months and years ahead. No one in our neighborhood had thought much about the effects of insecticide at that time, except my mother who often wondered aloud how something that so effectively killed insects could be benign to other living creatures. Rachel Carson published *Silent Spring* in 1962.

For more than thirty years Hattie supplemented their income with the private and commercial sale of those blueberries. When the berries were ripe, just prior to picking, several field workers laid rows of cotton twine in measured lines across the fields. Rows were a simple way to create boundaries within which the pickers raked.

Large vans arrived with pickers who'd been given rakes for harvesting the berries as quickly and efficiently as possible. A portable container was at the end of each row so pickers could dump their berries before the containers were picked up and brought to a central location. A winnower sorted debris and, after cleaning, the berries went to the canning factory for processing.

We, like most of Hattie's neighbors, looked forward to the day the van moved the professional pickers to the next site. This signaled that it was time for Hattie to open her fields to local pickers who paid her by the quart. I liked picking blueberries at Hattie's in spite of pesky yellow-jackets to watch for, brambles to climb through and steep terrain to climb. It was always worth the effort. I discovered early on that some of the best berries, silvery-blue and plump, grew beside granite boulders, where pickers hadn't found them or where they couldn't be reached with rakes if they had.

On one blistering, hot day I was picking berries at Hattie's with Mummy. She had found some berries not far from the parking area. I, on the other hand, spent about a third of my time running over the field, up and down, across rocks and briars, looking for the "best" berries. My search led me to two granite boulders at the edge of the woods. I couldn't believe my eyes! A cache of blueberry bushes that looked cultivated, their shiny green leaves nearly hidden behind the sea of blue. In the shade of those trees and boulders I picked all the berries I could carry in my two-gallon bucket.

Mummy was sorting out leaves and dried twigs from her berries when I reached her. We walked single file along the trampled path to the parking lot when Colby, a friend of Dad's, noticed us as he drove up Rice Hill. He was headed home to Freedom when he stopped his car and called out, "I see you been pickin' some berries!"

I held up my bucket for him to see.

"You prob'ly thought you was alone!"

"Mum and I were the only two ones picking today," I answered. Colby smiled. "Well, you wan't alone. I watched a big black bear pickin' right alongside you!"

I gasped then caught myself. "Are you teasing me?"

Colby made all he could of the moment. "You think I'd tease you about something as scary as a black bear?"

Mummy, who rarely responded to alarmist dialogue, calmly pointed out, "I wish I'd seen it! Blueberries are a main source of diet for black bears. It wouldn't have been interested in either one of us."

I looked at Mum. "Really? You'd like to have seen it... that close?"

Colby chortled. His intention to spook us had at least been halfway successful.

Zippoo, 1944

Porter Primary

I watched from the window as the school bus came into Kezar Falls village. Girls skipped and hopped, carefully avoiding the cracks in the sidewalk. I wondered what it would be like to walk to school.

As the bus approached Porter High School, the girl next to me gathered her books and lunch bag, but never stopped talking with her friend across the aisle. I was feeling anxious but followed Dad's instructions: I waited until the bus came to a stop before standing up to get off. When Mr. Carpenter, the bus driver, opened the bus door to let the older kids out, I clutched my lunch bag ready to get off too. From his rear view mirror Mr. Carpenter noticed me in line with the older kids but waited until I was standing closer to him to speak to me.

"You don't want to get off here, deah," he said kindly. "This is the high school. Our next stop will be Porter Primary. That's where you want to get off."

I was determined. "But Daddy said to get off when the bus stopped!" I wanted to cry.

Mr. Carpenter smiled.

"He meant for you to get off once the bus stopped at Porter Primary School."

I returned to my seat, even more anxious. Two minutes later we were in front of Porter Primary School. Mr.

Carpenter, looking into the rear view mirror said, "Now you can get off, deah!"

As my legs reached down the long steps of the yellow bus I was drawn into a crowd of children who, unlike me, seemed to know where they were going. Like many, I clutched a brown paper lunch bag, mine with a squished tomato sandwich. I looked around, trying to see what others were doing so I could figure out what I was supposed to do. I looked for a familiar face, but didn't find one. Most kids were taller and older than I.

They moved in a herd toward the school entrance before fanning out. Two older boys carried black lunch pails with thermos bottles that rattled when they jiggled their pails. I wanted to laugh but wasn't sure if I should; no one else was laughing. A girl smiled as she walked toward me and I noticed she didn't have a lunch bag.

"Where's your lunch?" I asked.

"Grammy lives down the street, so I'll go home or go to Grammy's for lunch," she said.

I overheard other kids talking about Sunday School, Sid Stanley's barn and swimming at Spec Pond—all things I was unfamiliar with, although I had heard of Sunday School, and Daddy sometimes went to Sid Stanley's barn.

––––––––

As we gathered in front of the doorway, a teacher in a black dress and black lace-up shoes stood on the front steps. She asked us to line up by grade, starting with sub-primary. When she reached into the neck opening of her dress and pulled out a handkerchief, I was incredulous. I'd never seen anyone pull a hanky from inside their dress before! I looked around to see if anyone had seen what I just saw.

"Where do I go?" I asked.

She placed her hand atop my head, let it slide down to my collar and pulled me to a short line at the far left. "You stay right here," she snapped. I swallowed hard, trying not to cry. *Why was she so mean? I'd only asked a simple question.* By this time I didn't like anything about Porter Primary School.

I noticed two more teachers standing on each side of the wide, open door. A younger teacher with curly brown hair spoke to us in a friendly voice. "Come in quietly, boys and girls. Boys, take off your caps. Keep your hands to yourselves."

Once inside, I detected a bad smell—like dirty rags. It made me feel queasy. I wrinkled up my face while glancing around to see if anyone else noticed the smell. *Was I the only one?*

The stairway that led up to the sub-primary and first-grade classrooms was straight ahead. As we lined up the teacher in black bent over with outstretched arms, reaching for anyone who strayed from the line.

"You children line up on the right side and walk quietly up the stairs to your classrooms. Second and Third Graders, go into your classrooms and find a seat," she said, her voice growing hoarse. At this point I'd been on the bus since 6:40 a.m., and no one had mentioned a bathroom. I worried that maybe there wasn't one.

Holding the railing as we climbed, the younger teacher made sure we stayed in line. "This is where you go to the basement," she said at the landing, pointing to a door on the second floor landing. *Basement? Up here? So confusing!*

When the young teacher called my name to go to the bathroom, I was so relieved that I barely had time to close the door behind me. I laid my lunch bag down on the oiled floor, pulled up my skirt and pulled down my panties before sitting on the black, wooden toilet seat. My feet dangled in the air as I peed beneath the light of a single light bulb dangling from the overhead fixture. *Why did she call the bathroom a basement?*

As I walked out of the bathroom the teacher pointed to a shorter set of stairs on the right, "Your room is at the top of the stairs," she said. I climbed the last set of stairs where an old lady greeted me with a warm smile. "Welcome to sub-primary," she said. "My name is Mrs. Stanley and, let me guess… you are Charlotte!"

"Yup."

I looked around the room and liked what I saw: a large sandbox with little cars, trucks and rubber farm animals; children's books; an easel with tempera paints; a piano; a play corner with dolls, a record player and a large blackboard with a chalk tray. There were four tables with four chairs at each table. As soon as all the children were in the room, Mrs. Stanley moved from the doorway to the front of the class. "Good morning, boys and girls. My name is Mrs. Stanley. Find a seat at a table, and please be seated."

When we were all settled she announced, "My name looks like this" and slowly wrote her name on the blackboard. "Now everyone, please stand then push in your chairs." She stood straight, looking up at the American flag with its 48 stars. With her right hand over her heart, she asked us to place our right hands over our hearts and repeat after her.

"I pledge allegiance… to the Flag … of the United States

of America... and to the Republic... for which it stands... one Nation... indivisible... with liberty... and justice for all."

She followed it with the Lord's Prayer.

Then the 23rd Psalm.

"You may be seated," she said. "Next, I'll write your name on the card you see on the table in front of you."

Some kids started talking, and she asked them to use quiet voices while she took attendance. *Attendance? What does that mean?*

After attendance Mrs. Stanley handed out soft-covered books for us to look through. The pictures in *We Look and See* showed a girl with yellow hair in a pink dress; a boy with light brown hair wearing brown shorts and a blue shirt; a white house; and a white picket fence around the house. I liked the pictures even though they didn't look anything like my family or our house.

"Can anyone read the first page?" our teacher asked.

"I can!" I answered.

"Can anyone else read the first page?" the teacher asked again. *I guess I'm not the only one who can read!*

Another hand went up as another "I can!" came from a voice at another table. She looked older, as tall as most of the boys. "What does the first word say?" asked the teacher.

"See."

"Next?"

"Dick," said another voice.

"And the next word?"

"Run!" I shouted. "See Dick run!"

"You're reading!" exclaimed Mrs. Stanley.

What I didn't know was that about half of the children in my class didn't have any books at home. Some might never have even seen a book until that day.

Recess on the playground was where social dramas played out in games of house, cowboys, mumbly peg, hopscotch and marbles. It's where an unspoken language was learned through observation, speaking, listening, smelling, tasting and touching.

Marbles was my favorite game. I loved competition and having marbles in my pocket. When two or three friends were standing around, one would suggest a game of marbles. After agreeing to play, one would dig their shoe heel into the ground to make a hole and, with the heel firmly in place, begin to turn in the same direction, around and around until the hole was deep and wide enough to hold plenty of marbles. Someone would draw a straight line, eight to ten feet away, and the game would begin once the number of marbles was agreed upon. Whoever got the most marbles in the pot with the fewest shots won the game. There were many nuances to the game—even different kinds of marbles.

At the rear of the building was an indentation known as the cubby, where seven or eight kids could meet at the same time. There was an unspoken rule that younger kids were not welcome; only the "Big Kids" (third graders) were allowed to meet there to discuss taboo subjects like sex. Being uninformed and curious we formed a club to report on sounds made by our parents when they were in bed. The cubby was a place where discoveries were made and secrets confided—but no one knew very much. A most exciting moment came when Janice said that her mother was going to have a baby.

When boys ganged up against the girls I sometimes wished to be on their side when the girls shrieked, pretending to be afraid.

It was in the cubby and on the ninety-minute bus rides that I gained understanding, albeit limited, of how to relate to my classmates. I learned many families lived tough lives that affected how they acted at school. There were some kids in my class who had no breakfast; others didn't have warm clothing. One woman with sixteen children rode the bus with us so she could get to her housekeeping job to feed her family. Her husband could no longer work in the woods because of a back injury, and their options were limited. When she stepped onto the bus, voices popped up all over the bus.

"Mummah, sit here!"

"Sit with me, Mummah! You sat with Bertha last time!"

Even those of us who weren't her children wanted her to sit with us. Her strength and kindness were felt by anyone in her presence.

Sometimes the cubby was a place where gossip was shared. After a few blunders I realized that everyone in town was related to everyone else, my family being one of only a few exceptions. I became ever so careful of who I spoke of and to whom!

Curtis Chick

Curtis was unforgettable—whether you remembered his kindness when he taught neighborhood children how to fish or his physical appearance, you would never forget him.

When the United States became engaged in WWI, Curtis was drafted to serve in the Army. Having rarely been beyond a thirty-mile radius, Curtis complied with his orders, but he had little or no concept of what he was getting into. He had no frame of reference for the war. Along with other draftees, Curtis found a ride to Portland and from there was transported with the other draftees to Fort Devens in Massachusetts for basic training.

Dad later explained to us that Curtis refused to shower communally with his regiment at boot camp, something all draftees were expected to do. Curtis continued to refuse and was discharged from the Army and spent the next twenty-five years at the Augusta Mental Health Institute tending apple, pear and peach orchards for the self-sufficient institution.

Curtis was released from AMHI in 1947 and assigned a guardian to pay his bills and attend to any legal matters. Eventually the U.S. government built him a standard ranch house, beside his old house. He was never consulted but accepted the new house that would require only minimum maintenance. Occasionally Curtis would ask Dad to intervene when he felt he was being taken advantage of, especially around matters of land boundaries and ownership. He was more comfortable talking to my father than to his guardian. Dad did what he could to help Curt untangle and understand legal issues with his deeds and to make certain Curt was treated fairly.

Curt would walk to our house to ask Daddy for legal and financial advice. "Nawdo, see here, don't-cha-know," What they want to do is... what can you do about this," he'd say.

Daddy would read over the document Curt handed over. "Curt, I'm no banker or lawyer, but I'll see what I can to help you." And Daddy did help him, many times. He would drop anything he was doing for Curt's peace of mind.

Following Dad's example, I learned to respect and cherish Curtis for the kind and gentle man he was. Curtis shared his vast knowledge of fishing and gardening with his neighbors, most of whom lived in a faster-paced world, far outside his frame of reference. Curt clearly identified with his Pequawket heritage, as evidenced by the way he lived.

I don't recall ever seeing Curt without a corncob pipe, spittle running down the side of his mouth and a twinkle in his eye. He spit out the brown juice wherever he was, wiped his mouth on his crusted sleeve, and began in a slow but animated drawl, "Ya know, Nawdo..."

Curt spoke as though no air passed through his nostrils, and since he smoked his pipe more or less constantly, it's possible the air couldn't pass through. In spite of his inattention to personal hygiene, he was respected and cherished by most who knew him.

When people met Curtis for the first time they were often so appalled by his personal appearance that they neglected to see the person behind the scruffy beard, filthy long johns and tobacco-stained shirt. They might also have been put off by his scratching of his upper body.

Curtis walked where he needed to go on well-worn paths his ancestors used, shortcuts to his destinations. He stashed Narragansett bottles beside boulders along the way, where there was only the slightest chance his beer would be pilfered since his paths led to places few, if any, would ever go.

One such path led over steep terrain of Kennard Hill to the Sargents' farm in Freedom, just over the state line. Once a month Hattie Sargent drove Curtis to Goodwin's in Kezar Falls for his monthly supply of groceries and anything else he needed. Goodwin's also sold work boots, shoes, men's caps and hunting outfits. Hattie and Curtis returned home via Andy's, a small variety store that specialized in beer, just over the New Hampshire line in Freedom.

———

When Curtis was in his late seventies he offered to show our family the cellar hole that remained where his family's homestead once stood. Dad took him up on his offer in early May, before the black flies had hatched. Curtis waited for us on his stoop, tapping his corncob pipe against the cement before reaching into his shirt pocket for more tobacco.

"Nawdo," he said, smiling. He had changed from his winter uniform of red-and-black plaid wool to his spring outfit: loose denim jeans held up with a long leather belt and a faded chambray shirt over his union suit. He hadn't yet parted with his leather work boots crusted in mud.

Curt rose slowly and walked down the cement steps, holding onto the wrought iron railing. He acknowledged us with a nod of his head as he strode toward Mum and Dad. "Curt, are you still up to taking a walk to the cellar hole?" Dad asked.

Curt's wrinkled face beamed as he replied, "It's up on the Old Varney Road, don't-cha-know." He stood, as he often did, with his legs crossed, occasionally moving his head forward then sideways to spit chewing tobacco juice. In silence he started walking toward the road with Dad by his side. Mum walked with us, a few paces behind.

Once we crossed the road and walked a few yards on Danforth Lane, we turned onto the Varney Road, a discontinued town road between Kennard Hill Road and Colcord Pond Road. As we ambled along Curt pointed out plants and birds. He plucked five young beech leaves, still tightly curled, from a young tree, and handed us each one to chew on. "See why deer like 'em?"

"They taste like fresh peas," I noted.

Curt continued, "See those beech branches? You can see where deer nipped off the buds. They eat a lot of beech buds in the spring."

"Can we get some more?" I asked.

"Best to get them from a different tree," he said.

I plucked six leaves from another young beech beside the road, enough for my sisters and me to have two more, but not enough to harm the tree.

"Mummy, do you want to try some?" Kathy asked.

"Dear, you've aroused my curiosity," she said. "Sure, I'll try one."

Kathy handed Mummy one of her leaves.

"These taste familiar," she said, "very much like fresh peas!"

"I'll pick some more." I suggested and ran to another tree.

Meanwhile, Dad and Curt were getting farther ahead.

"We'd better wait to get our beech leaves on the way back. We need to catch up, or Curt will be ready to leave before we even get there!" I said, walking faster to catch up.

The road was muddy as we climbed to the top of the hill at the base of Bald Ledge. Curt stood facing the cellar hole. "I was born here," he said and spit tobacco juice onto his foot.

As we milled about I noticed a small white button with two holes on the ground. I reached down and picked it up. When I straightened, Curtis gave me a look I would never forget.

"Leave that here. It belonged to Mother," he said calmly.

Feeling ashamed, I promptly laid the button back among the pine needles. We continued on the Varney Road, turning left onto Breakneck Hill Road and right onto the road that led to the heath (once an important trading site for local tribes). Curtis pronounced it hāth so we did too.

As we approached the heath, we heard the loud slap of a beaver tail hitting the water. Then another. Beavers had built a dam close to the opening by the road where the grassy wetland extended for eighty-seven acres. This wetland provided a source of drinking water for many species of animals and was home to wild cranberries and blueberries. Curt's deep reverence for this place was evident by the respect he conveyed as he reminisced about the heath's importance to his own family.

———

Curtis's father, Still Chick, was a skilled boat builder who occasionally left his family to travel to the coast for work. Curtis had a sister, Viola and a brother, Howard who was as unlike Curtis as you could imagine. Viola was painfully shy around strangers but often accompanied Curtis on evenings of hornpouting in their wooden boat, kept on the shore of Bickford Pond.

When weather conditions were favorable they walked through the woods to the northern end of Bickford where they fished for hornpout, pickerel and perch. This was such an evening.

Though the sun had set, there was still enough light for them to see the path leading to the shore, where, under swooping hemlock branches, they kept a faded green, flat-bottomed boat, inverted on two oak logs.

Viola picked her way along the path behind Curtis, her graying hair in a loose knot in back with a few loose strands clinging to the cheekbones of her deeply lined face. Both her dress and apron were sewn from floral-printed grain sacks by Hattie, their neighbor on the New Hampshire side of the border. Viola, painfully shy, trusted few people, with the exceptions of Curtis and Hattie.

Curtis, tall and lean, wore the same denim jeans he'd had on for months, possibly years! His long-sleeved undershirt worn beneath a stained, blue chambray shirt, was loosely tucked into his jeans and secured with a worn leather belt. He held his corncob pipe loosely between his teeth as he fetched the oars and oarlocks hidden nearby while Viola held the lantern. Curtis righted the boat and pulled it into the water, steadying the boat at the water's edge while Viola grabbed hold of the gunnels, lifted her dress and climbed aboard.

The remaining glow on the western hills faded, sliding the valley into darkness. Lifting the chimney of his kerosene lantern, Curtis adjusted the wick and flicked his thumbnail against the wooden match to light the wick, then handed the lantern to Viola. Before getting into the boat himself, he clipped a willow branch to hold their evening's catch, while Viola put the lantern down to help Curtis bring aboard the long bamboo poles they stored under their boat.

They said little during this ritual of many decades. One night when it was getting dark we heard Curtis slide the oars into the oar locks then row steadily and quietly to the spot in the cove where he knew there would be hornpout, a few perch—possibly, an eel. He lowered an anchor of stone, bound by clothesline, until it hit the bottom at about fourteen feet.

The stillness of night was interrupted occasionally by the screeching of barred owls, a chorus of bullfrogs in Douglas Cove and rustling of branches near Pearl Brook.

"Did you hear the barred owl? Listen!" I urged.

"I hear the owl and the bullfrogs too!" my friend Bobby said, imitating their chuga-rum, chuga-rum.

"Shh-hh, Curtis and Viola are probably wishing you'd stop chuga-rumming," I whispered.

Curtis and Viola fished in silence, occasionally pulling in a hornpout or perch. By ten o'clock they laid down their bamboo poles, and Curtis rowed back to shore. They'd caught enough fish to feed themselves and their cats for another week.

Once ashore, Curtis climbed out, then steadied the boat for Viola as she stepped out with the willow branch, laden with their evening's catch. She carefully laid the fish on the ground to help Curtis haul the boat up. Together they turned it over and stowed it beneath the hemlock, placing the poles underneath. Viola dragged the willow branch through the water, back and forth, to wash off any dirt that had collected on the fish while she and Curtis hid the oars.

Dark clouds formed, blocking stars in the western sky. Curtis's kerosene lantern would guide their slow, steady pace home.

Hattie Sargent's burial in Brownfield was a dramatic day with black clouds racing across the sky with sun streaking through. Curtis stood on the periphery of the cemetery, his arm draped over a fence post for stability. He stood out as the distinguished sage he was. For this special occasion he was clean shaven, wearing a wool-tweed coat and wide-brimmed felt hat—a most alluring figure against the dramatic backdrop of roiling black clouds.

Curtis died a few weeks shy of his 100th birthday in a nursing home, over an hour from his home.

Digging to China

Thousands of white pine seedlings had been planted by Manny in what had been rugged, sloping pasture across the road from our home. "Hard scrabble" comes to mind when describing this land. The soil of this steep moraine was littered with rocks of all sizes, from pebbles to boulders, and home to native plants, including mayflowers, trillium, checkerberry, jack-in-the-pulpit, and bellwort.

The pine plantation on this hillside was a favorite place for Kathy and me to play and where we visited the cemetery overlooking the valley below. Once, while scraping the lichen from the headstones, I noted that none of the children buried there had lived to be ten.

———

Some weeks later, while riding home on the school bus, I overheard older kids talking about China, a place that sparked my interest, so I listened intently. One of them said that if he were to dig to the other side of the Earth he would eventually come out in China. I couldn't wait to tell Bobby and didn't want to wait a minute longer than I had to. China was a place I'd read about in children's books, a place I wanted to know more about, especially Chinese kites, Chinese costumes and Chinese pork.

Mummy had read to us a Chinese children's tale about

a fire in a Chinese village. A little boy walking past a burned pig noticed a delicious aroma coming from the pig. The boy stopped, walked over to the pig, poked his finger into the pig's burned flesh and removed his finger, then licked it. It was so delicious he did it again and again. He'd discovered something truly special. According to the Chinese tale, this is how roast pork came to be discovered. And I loved to eat.

I was ready to start digging on the hill across the road because Daddy had said it was easier for Manny to plant the pines in the sandy soil on the hill than anywhere else, because there were fewer rocks.

One morning in early May, with my chores finished and the sun shining, I had a mission! From the bottom of the stairs I called to Mummy who was making beds upstairs, "May I go to the cemetery on the hill... across the road?"

She came to the head of the stairs, "You'd better put on some fly dope before you go. The black flies are apt to be out in swarms since it's supposed to rain later this afternoon. Be back in time for lunch."

I found the Ole Woodsman's fly dope and spread it over my arms and legs and behind my ears, being careful not to get it in my eyes.

Carrying the smallest spade I could find, I crossed the dirt road and climbed the banking on the path that went to a natural spring on the hillside. This was where the water we used to drink, cook, bathe, wash dishes and do laundry began its journey through copper piping buried in a three-foot-deep trench. With gravity, the water flowed from the spring through the pipes, into our home. All we had to do was turn on a faucet.

Halfway to the spring I looked to see if the cemetery was within sight and could just barely see the granite fence through the new foliage, so I veered off the path, stumbling over dead branches and laid down my spade before walking to an outcropping. There I could see my house directly below. It looked so different. *A bird's eye view!* Looking beyond, across the valley, Black Mountain was a patchwork of tints and shades of green.

A clearing opened up just below the cemetery. I picked up my spade and walked on a carpet of gold-orange pine needles, down an incline, to a sunny spot with fewer trees. *This is where I'll dig!* I drove my spade into the sandy soil and emptied the sand as far away from the hole as I could reach. I repeated the digging, lifting and emptying, until the hole was almost as deep as I was tall. As I dug around the edges to widen the hole so I could get out I noticed long, white hair-like strands scattered throughout the sand.

Daddy had reminded me the night before that I must never dig in a cemetery. *At least I wasn't in a cemetery!* He'd also mentioned that Curt Chick thought there was an Indian burial site on this very hill. Because Curt didn't know just where it was, Daddy didn't know either. *Could the long white strands belong to an Indian?* That thought was especially disturbing because I knew how upset Daddy would be with me.

It crossed my mind that I might be getting close to China, and that the white hair-like strands might possibly be Chinese hair. *Should I keep digging and risk having Dad know that I dug up hair, or should I just leave, right away?* In a split second I was on my way down—straight down the hill, dragging the spade behind me.

The last time I walked up that hill was ten years ago,

when I was 73. The hole is still there but now filled with debris from the pines Manny planted a century ago.

Pine Plantation

He's out in the barn

Brownfield Fire

When the Brownfield fires raged in 1947, I was just six years old. The crimson sky that October night haunts me still. The fire incinerated most homes in Brownfield Village and was moving southeast, toward our home in Porter. We were prepared to evacuate as fire trucks rumbled by carrying water and firefighters to Brownfield.

The day before, Mummy left by train to attend her father's funeral in Boston. The timing couldn't have been worse. Fires blazed throughout Maine, and the train Mummy was on passed *through* the fire in Waterboro, something I overheard Daddy talking with her about on the telephone.

Gram Hadlock was helping Kathy and me round up laundry when we heard frantic knocking on the front door. I ran to open the door and was startled to see a fire warden standing there. "Is your Daddy at home?" he asked. "I'd like to speak to him."

"He's out in the barn, but I can get him."

"That sure would be helpful," he said.

I raced to the barn to find Daddy collecting shovels, a pick-ax and a regular ax. "Daddy, there's a man in a uniform in the vestibule. He wants to speak with you."

Dad hurried back to the house ahead of me to meet with the fire warden. "Ken, I've been collecting what tools

I have that would be helpful to fight the fire."

"Joe, we need all the volunteers we can round up to help us battle the fire. It's destroying everything in its path, and it's headed in this direction. It's so goddamn dry that a single spark will set off a blaze that will be out of control in no time."

While Dad didn't want to burden Gram with the full responsibility of his children, this was no ordinary time. Gram encouraged him to go, assuring him she'd manage just fine.

Ken added, "We need strong men who can fight this terrible fire. The ground is so dry the fire is traveling along root systems. Cutting away roots and digging trenches should slow the fire. We'll see."

Not surprisingly, we were all scared. In preparation for the worst, Dad gave us each a bag and helped us select a few essential clothes and belongings. Revy had her own packed bag and was prepared to take Kathy and me to the lake where we'd row away from shore if necessary. Since Louise was so young and Gram was so old, they would stay home together until Dad returned to take them to safety, should the fire keep coming in our direction.

———————

Early the next morning Dad gathered Kathy and me in his arms before he left. He then picked Louise up, held her high in the air and gave her a gentle "cheek to cheek." He told us that Gram would be with us, that he would be leaving us to fight the fire—and he'd be back as soon as he could. "You girls be helpful to Gram. *Stang gamba.*"

Dad always said that when he wanted us to be brave. Out of curiosity I once looked it up. *Gamba* means "leg" in

Italian. *Stang* means rod in German. I suspect he thought it meant "stand strong" because of the context in which he used it.

When it was apparent that the Brownfield Fire wasn't going to be easily stopped, the Ladies Auxiliary set up a feeding station in our kitchen. Cold cuts, sliced cheese, loaves of white bread, mustard, donuts, freshly brewed coffee, cookies, apples and candy bars.

Exhausted firefighters took breaks, ate their fill, quenched their thirst and some even caught a few hours of sleep in our guest room. The commotion was both scary and exciting. So many people coming and going.

The evening after Brownfield Village was ravaged, Dad checked in on us then made himself a sandwich. He brought me outside to look at the night sky, a surreal deep red-orange. Glowing, acorn-sized embers fell to the parched earth. I knew Dad was scared because he talked to me as though I were a grown-up. He hooked the garden hose to an outside spigot and showed me how to direct the water stream to wet down the roof. I loved being able to help my Dad. *Does he expect me to save the house?!*

While we soaked the roof, Chet Cutting stopped to say that the wind had shifted and was no longer moving in our direction. With a hint of optimism Dad said, "Let's hope the wind is blowing toward an area that's already burned."

————

The 1947 fire burned 21,120 acres in Brownfield alone. Even a hint of wood smoke wafting through the air still sends me into a high alert.

Epiphany

It was a day that prompted Mummy to say, "We must get the good of the day!"

Mare's tails streaked above the southern horizon, while overhead the sky was a deep cerulean blue, making me wish I could fly above the fields, riding the air currents like a red-tailed hawk.

In just two weeks I'd be going to second grade, so I was making the most of my last weeks of summer, walking carefree through Rev and Manny's field before paying them a visit. Shoots of bright green timothy poked up amongst the dry stubble left after haying the second crop. I was going to see if there were any apples on the three apple trees Manny had planted on the north side of the field, at the edge of the pine plantation.

The only apple tree with a branch I could reach was laden with butternut-sized green apples. I picked a small, imperfect one and turned it over and around in my hand, looking for any sign of worm holes; finding none, I took a bite. *Eeew!* I spit out the apple and threw the rest into the field as far as I could throw.

I looked up, wondering if my grandmother Charlotte might be able to see me. She died well before I was born, but Mummy and Rev told stories about her that made me wish I could have known her. I thought about her from time to time and wondered if she knew of my existence. Our Sunday School by Mail with Rev taught us that heaven was above the earth, so my grandmother might be there, looking down, able to see me.

I felt close to her as I peered into the boundless blue space above, wondering about heaven when I noticed tiny circular specks wherever I looked. I kept looking at them, thinking of my grandmother. Then it came to me: Those specks were angels! My mind raced with excitement. I dallied in the field, hoping my grandmother would send me a message. If she did, I missed it, but I was convinced I'd discovered where angels resided.

The Moutons

From a young age I became increasingly aware of how differently my family and the Moutons lived. The Moutons lived to have FUN! My family lived to work, or so it seemed. Living on a farm, even a quasi-farm like ours, meant there was always work to be done.

That said, I never wished that we lived the way they did. Though our families were on good terms, I never thought to ask my parents why they never invited the Moutons to come for dinner—or why my parents weren't among the adults sitting on the dock with cold drinks. I must have known intuitively that my parents, Mum in particular, would've been uncomfortable. I'm pretty sure the Moutons understood this as well. As different as they were, our parents accepted one another.

Buster and Ada worked eight hour days, five days a week, at the Portsmouth Naval Shipyard where Ada was secretary to the shipyard Commander, and Buster was Chief Electrician. Their jobs must have suited them, as I never heard either of them complain about their work. Rather, the shipyard was not only a means to good times, it became the focal point of their social life.

In the 1940s and early 1950s there were few women naval officers in the United States, none of whom were stationed at the Portsmouth Navy Yard. If they were there, they weren't among the officers who came to the Moutons' camp.

In summertime, as soon as Buster and Ada left work on Friday afternoons, not wanting to waste a minute, they scooped up Ada's mother Gram Blazo, my friend Bobby and Pete, their guinea pig, and headed to their camp, stopping along the way for groceries and gas. It was a rare weekend when they didn't have guests, mostly officers at the shipyard. Their camp provided a relaxing change of venue: boats, water skis, fishing gear, swimming and plenty of food. The Moutons were generous hosts. They were also generous to their neighbors, sharing bounty from their garden, oysters when Buster harvested them and hornpout after a good catch.

Some years during winter vacations, when they were feeling especially flush, Buster and Ada vacationed in Havana where they feasted on Cuban food, drank Cuban rum and danced to Afro-Cuban jazz until wee hours of the morning while Bobby and Gram stayed at home with Pete.

Buster's childhood was colorful but not easy. He spent most of his youth with his flamboyant and undependable father in Lafayette, Louisiana, occasionally visiting his unstable mother in Portsmouth. On one of these visits Buster had the good fortune to meet the Dores, a family from Portsmouth. They quickly bonded, and soon the Dores were treating Buster like an adopted son—even taking him to their cottage on Lake Winnipesaukee for summer vacation. "The Dores were good people," Buster said on more than one occasion. "Salt of the earth."

Buster was 5'5", of medium build and proud of his position as chief electrician at the Portsmouth Naval Shipyard. He loved to talk about "The Yard" with anyone who would listen. It didn't matter how many times he'd told them the same story—as long as they were willing to listen! It helped that Buster was a good storyteller, never shying away from embroidering a few of the details.

Not only handy with wood and anything electrical, Buster liked to cook, but only his favorite foods: grilled steak, crispy french fries and tossed green salad. When living with his father in New Orleans, Buster had developed a fondness for French cooking because of one of its secrets: an abundance of butter! He took that secret to heart. He also had an audacious streak that could be entertaining... or dangerous, depending on the situation. He was known to check whether an electrical wire was "live" by licking the tips of his thumb and index finger before grabbing the wire. I had trouble believing this until I watched him as he exclaimed, "She's hot!"

Buster treated Ada "like royalty," as she liked to say. Because she had phlebitis and leg ulcers she spent most of her time in a reclining chair, at home or at camp. Beside the large window overlooking the pond, she did crossword puzzles and entertained neighbors, young and old. In between visitors, she checked on Buster as he fished for salmon. Or she spoke with Lucy, her friend at the other end of the pond. Since they were on a five-party line, neighbors were known to listen in on other neighbors' conversations, and Ada was no exception. Meanwhile, Gram puttered in the kitchen, washed underwear and bandages and brought them out to dry on the clothesline.

Gram Blazo lived with the Moutons and assisted with cooking and household chores, but most importantly, she acted as a sage. Gram offered judicious advice and was treasured by those who appreciated her irreverence, wit and dry sense of humor. Physically, she was petite, dressed in brown cotton stockings, a starched housedress, starched apron and, always, comfy slippers. Her white hair, loosely pinned in a bun, accentuated her sagging jowls. Even the slightest provocation would draw a quick, snake-like motion of her tongue and brighten her taciturn expression.

Rumor had it that as a young woman once or twice a week Gram climbed into her harness-racing sulky to exercise her stallion by driving him, in any kind of weather, down what is now Route 25 from Porter Village to Cornish and back—twelve miles in all. She was a lot tougher than she looked!

Shucking Oysters

The loggers' cast-iron wood stove was the prominent feature in our kitchen. Four-feet long and four-and-a-half feet tall, it welcomed anyone who entered with its warmth; or as a point of conversation when it wasn't lit. Mum baked corn puddings, roasted chickens and beef, simmered delectable pot roasts and even baked a few pies in that oven. Nonna had given Mum and Dad a large, handsome teakettle from Italy, and it simmered on top of the stove, ready for anyone who wanted a cup of tea. Wood to feed the fire was stored in the woodbox, in the narrow space behind the stove. Mum kept a couple of cast-iron skillets at the rear of the stove for frying eggs, red-flannel hash and much, much more.

As we grew, Mummy's interest in cooking also grew. She became determined to bake real French bread, and she succeeded beyond her expectations. This success led my parents to indulge in buying a bright red Chambers gas stove that was installed within five feet of the wood stove. Its precise oven temperature control proved to be irreplaceable.

Buster Mouton dropped by early one afternoon on his way to camp, setting a basket of freshly harvested oysters down by the woodstove to warm his aching hands, still cold from being out on Great Bay Estuary in New Hampshire earlier in the day. He dragged a chair from the dining room table to be closer to the stove, but before he sat down he took his pointed shucking knife from its sheath in his basket and a lidded jar for the shucked oysters. "Say, you got a bucket I could use for the shells. And a towel... you don't mind gettin' a little mud on 'er do you, Nawdo?"

Dad was in the kitchen pouring Buster "a short one." He stooped down and reached into the kitchen cupboard beneath the sink and pulled out the aluminum pot that was used for extra compost in the summertime. "This okay, Bus?" he said, pulling a dish towel from the drying rack behind the wood stove, handing the pot and towel to Buster.

"You won't forget the brandy will you, Nawdo?" Buster mused, with a glint in his eyes and a devilish grin. "Them oysters go down awful easy with a little brandy."

Mummy retreated to her bailiwick, as she referred to the back room where she read and had her desk and easy chair. She had little interest in listening to stories of The Yard.

Back in the kitchen, Buster was excitedly telling a story. "You know, Nawdo, we're lucky this basket of oysters got here at all. Down in the bay, we was reachin' overboard when we see this boat speedin' toward us. I knew we'd better get rid o' the rum, but rather than waste it, I told Ralph to sit on it. When the game warden asked to see what was in our basket, I reached for it so Ralph wouldn't have to. 'Only a few oysters; that's it.' I said. The game warden, he seemed pretty satisfied, but I had a feelin' he knew we had some booze. I kept talking—you know, to distract him—so he wouldn't look at Ralph. 'Remember the limit!' the game warden hollered as he shoved the engine into gear and sped off—toward Newington. I remembered the limit all right, but that didn't mean that I'd do as he'd say! He said to remember the limit, not to obey the limit. There's a big difference!"

Buster chortled as tears rolled down his face.

He loved his own stories as much as we loved hearing them—the first time!

My sisters and I half-listened to Buster's "yarns" as we wandered in and out of the kitchen, stopping every so often to watch the production of oyster shucking, a ritual as basic for Buster as peeling onions. Holding each oyster with a towel, he slipped the knife between the shells at the hinge; then he gently wiggled the knife back and forth until the shells began to part. Slowly, he gave a slight twist of the knife, being careful not to cut into the oyster, which was attached to the top and bottom shells. He then scraped the oyster onto the bottom shell with his special knife, tossed the top shell into the pot, being careful not to spill the briny oyster liquor. With the shell in his hand Buster tipped his head back, parted his lips just wide enough to receive the slimy oyster as it slid into his mouth. With sounds of utter satisfaction, the slippery grayish mass slid down his gullet. "Here, you wanna try one!" he said, grinning, as he prepared the next oyster.

"Yee-uck," I replied with a grimace.

"You don't know what you're missing!" *Oh, yes I do.*

Dad mixed up a hot sauce mixture of chili sauce, horseradish and Tabasco. I never saw Buster chew an oyster; he simply held the oysters in their layered shells slightly above his mouth, tipped back his head and let the bivalves slide into his mouth. Dad liked the hot sauce, but I don't think he was wild about raw oysters.

Mummy entered the kitchen, looked at her watch, put

on her apron, and said, "Oh my, time escaped me. I must start dinner, but first let me put some wood on the fire."

"Alice, can I interest you in some of these?" Buster asked, holding up an oyster.

Mummy wasn't a fan of anything that needed as much preparation in the way of shucking and condiment-making. "Thank you Buster, but you save the oysters for those of you who savor them. I've never been a fan of raw oysters."

Dad was cleaning up the kitchen while Buster continued to tell stories about his work at the Navy Yard.

"Bus, you can leave the shells. I'll crush them and feed them to the hens. They can always use some extra calcium."

"You sure, Nawdo?"

"Leave 'em right there in the pot and I'll take care of them after supper."

Mummy sat at the dining room table while Buster cleaned up in the kitchen sink. She was ready to prepare supper of leftover pork shoulder, corn pudding and sautéed cabbage. Buster finally returned the chair to the table, buttoned up his red and black plaid wool shirt and collected his belongings. "These oysters are going to make one tasty stew. Too bad I'll have to have it all to myself. You folks have a good evening. Thanks for the brandy, Nawdo!"

It was almost dark as he stepped out of the vestibule with his jar of shucked oysters.

Preparing for France, 1950

As an eight-year-old, taking French lessons had not been on my list of priorities. But when Manny asked if I'd like to study French with him after school, I eagerly accepted even though I had no idea what it would entail.

Manny promised a "surprise" if I learned to speak and write French. It was the lure of that surprise that propelled me to accept. As a seven-year-old child I would never have contradicted Manny—nor rejected his wishes. Too often I'd seen his temper flare when Rev couldn't perform a task with the finesse he expected.

While Manny's faith in me was affirming, it also caused problems at home: Dad wanted me to spend more time with our family. I sensed his displeasure in his creased eyes and tight lips as I prepared for my daily walks to the Raffy's. My mother, on the other hand, felt different. As a child, Mummy studied French with Manny. She spoke French beautifully and was delighted to see me running to the Raffy's.

During late summer, just prior to entering third grade, Manny made a deal with me: that I would be rewarded if I studied French with him every day after school, learning to speak and write French well enough to communicate effectively.

I had little or no idea what I was getting myself into.

With the beginning of school in September, as soon as I stepped off the school bus in the afternoon, I wasted no time changing into my play clothes (even though I wasn't going outside to play). On my way out the door I grabbed a cookie and a glass of milk Mummy or Gram had left for me, then ran through the woods to the Raffy's for my French lesson.

As predictable as mayflowers in early spring, Manny would be sitting in his Morris chair, beside the fireplace, regardless of the season or what was happening around him. After giving Rev and Manny pecks on their soft, wrinkled cheeks, I sat down opposite Manny, ready to begin my lesson.

When the sun had set behind Black Mountain to the west, Rev lit the kerosene lamps in the living room and kitchen, where she puttered, preparing their simple evening meal. As the wood fire in the kitchen stove burned down, Rev lifted the iron lid with the lifter and slid pieces of split hardwood into the firebox, replaced the lid and adjusted the damper on the stove pipe to moderate the temperature.

My French lessons lasted for an hour, or more, depending on how Manny (and I) were feeling. Throughout my lessons he consistently spoke in French, as he always had; but now I paid closer attention, determined to learn to speak and write French—at any cost.

Looking back, I'd describe Manny as methodical and linear in everything he did. Manny also understood the importance of involving one's senses in order to learn more completely. It's the sensory experiences that I remember most vividly.

He pored over illustrated maps of France telling me stories related to historical points of interest and places he'd known; he read *Le Petit Prince* and Tintin books with me, and as much as I enjoyed being read to, the Tintin stories, in particular, were over my head, but the drawings delighted me to no end. I can still conjure an image of Tintin with papers flying through the air!

Music was also part of my sensory experience as Rev played "Au Claire de la Lune" and other French tunes, on the piano while I sang along with her, mostly off-key. She was so pleased that I was singing, she kept her criticisms to herself. During the Christmas season Rev opened a tin of paté de foie gras with truffles, made by Madame Dauphia. It took weeks for the package to arrive, but it was always worth the wait. Little did I know that in a few months I'd be helping Madame Dauphia feed the geese whose liver was being used to make the paté.

When Manny was describing perfume making in France he asked Rev to dab some lavender eau de toilette on my neck so that I could smell of lavender as Rev did from the lavender-scented hankie she kept tucked inside her bra.

Daddy suggested that I use his typewriter to write out verb declensions; that made learning the verbs ever so much easier. Plus, I was also learning to type, slowly but surely. Manny liked the orderliness of the typed pages with verbs declined beneath the headings.

By April of 1950, I had fulfilled my part of the deal, and Manny was rewarding me with a trip to France which he had prearranged with Mummy, in spite of Daddy's qualms. Ultimately, when presented with the choice to go or not to go, I chose to go. I had a passport with my picture grinning at whoever opened the document. Mummy had helped me choose two suitable, all-occasion dresses, sandals and a spring jacket. I insisted on packing my favorite pullover, a gray-blue sweater with a blue heron on the front along with shorts, tee shirts, socks and underwear.

A few days before Mummy and I left by train for New York with Manny, Dad called me aside to say he had something special for me. He handed me a small box. "Go ahead and open it carefully," he said, placing the box on the arm of his chair. In slow motion I reached inside and lifted out a small, but sturdy case. Then I slowly lifted its cover. "Daddy! A Mickey Mouse watch with a red leather strap!" I shrieked. "I can't believe it!"

"Go ahead, take it out of the case," Daddy urged. As I lifted up the watch and undid the strap, Daddy reminded me that it needed to be wound each day. "Like this," he said, taking the watch crown between his thumb and forefinger, moving it slowly back and forth. "Give it ten winds, that should be plenty. If it feels tight, stop, and whatever you do, don't force it!"

Daddy showed me how to bend my left elbow as he lay the watch across my arm, with the watch face in the middle, just above my wrist. I had trouble holding the watch in place until Daddy put the end of the strap through the buckle. "Now hold it against your chest while you slip the pin into the hole on the strap... where it feels comfortable."

It was clear to me: I would have to practice putting on my watch alone, over and over until I mastered it. I felt better when Dad explained, "The leather strap is stiff because it's new, but as you wear it it will soften." When I finally had the watch securely on my arm, I looked down at Mickey with his wide smile, his arms extended into his oversized yellow-gloves with the index finger pointing to the numbers.

"Will you show me how to set the time?" I asked. Dad looked at his watch. With a sheepish grin, he said, "I was waiting for you to ask!" He held the crown and gently pulled out the stem, setting the time. He moved Mickey's gloves and asked me to reset it after he'd pushed the crown back in place.

I followed Daddy's instructions and managed to set the time on the first try. "That wasn't hard," I bragged. Dad reminded me, "And one more thing before I go to the farm. You mustn't let the watch get wet." He couldn't resist telling me that he had chosen the watch because it would come in handy on my trip. He stopped for a minute, then added soulfully, "I hope you'll think of me whenever you look at your watch."

I could tell that Daddy was already missing me, and I hadn't even left yet. I gave Daddy a big hug, then I looked at my watch, and a grin stretched across my face. Dad got up to leave, and I was so overjoyed I exclaimed, "I can't wait to show Mummy!" I said, bounding upstairs to Louise's room where Mummy was helping Louise get dressed.

Once Daddy had left to go to the farm I asked Mummy if I could go to Rev and Manny's to show them my watch. She answered, "Well, I don't see why not, as long as your chores are done. And if you'd wait until Dad comes back from the farm with the milk, you'd save Dad some time if you would bring their milk to them."

"Okay. I'll wait," I said, glancing at my watch. "I'll see how long it takes Daddy to get here."

Daddy soon returned with two aluminum milk containers, with covers and handles. The half-gallon container was ours, and I carried the quart container to Rev and Manny's, walking along the edge of the road, being careful to keep the container upright.

I entered through the Raffy's back door and tiptoed into the living room where Rev was playing the piano. Manny was sitting in his chair, smoking and reading a French journal. When Manny heard the floor creak he looked up to see me standing in front of him, *"J'ai quelque chose à vous montrer,"* I said, moving my arm up across my chest to display the watch. Manny reacted: *"Qu'avons-nous ici? Tu es une publicité ambulante pour Monsieur Disney!"*

Rev stopped playing when she heard him comment that I was a walking commercial for Monsieur Disney. I was crushed—not only because I loved the watch, but especially since Daddy had given it to me. I fought back tears as Rev turned to me from the piano bench, asking me to come closer so that she could see it for herself. I held out my left arm for her to see. "You might have difficulty seeing what numbers Mickey's gloves are pointing to," she said, "But it will be nice to have a watch on your trip."

"I can see the numbers. I can tell you what time it is right now! 10:45. Daddy gave it to me for my trip."

In just a few days Manny, Mummy and I would be leaving for New York on the train, and I'd be able to keep track of the time.

———

Mummy and I spent the night in a Pullman sleeping car. According to my diary, she slept while I looked out the window "all night long." Manny spent the night in the regular passenger car. Knowing that Mummy would be left behind made me feel sad, but I was so glad to be with her on the first leg of our trip, from Portland to New York City.

The following day Manny and I would be boarding the *Île de France* in New York Harbor, and travel across the Atlantic to Le Havre. The crossing would take six days.

Once we were standing in the midst of Grand Central Station, crowds were scurrying to board trains and get to their destinations. I kept looking up, never having been in a space so large—so high. My view of the world was expanding.

Mummy and I had the entire morning to do as we pleased since Manny and I wouldn't be boarding the *Île de France* until later that afternoon. Knowing my interests, Mummy knew that I'd enjoy visiting the Museum of Natural History, which is where we spent the morning. From the minute we encountered a huge, life-size wooly mammoth, I was awe-struck! But of the exhibits we visited, my favorites were the dioramas of American mammals in their natural habitats; I wasn't sure the buffalo weren't going to come to life and burst through the glass case!

When we came out of the museum Mummy and I were ready to sit after standing for more than two hours. We settled on a park bench to watch gray squirrels scurry, hoping for food. When a squirrel finally dared jump onto our bench, I squealed with delight. I loved being in New York City, though it was clear that I was not a city girl.

Manny, meanwhile, had been waiting in Grand Central Station with our luggage, reading the daily papers and smoking Chesterfields. When we finally met up with him, it was time to take a taxi to the harbor where boarding of the *Île de France* was soon to begin. With passports in hand, passengers lined up. Mummy was lined up to come on board with us to see Manny and me off on our three-and-a-half-month adventure.

Alice, Front Row Center Right

SS Île de France

The minute I stepped aboard the ship, its rolling motion sent waves of nausea surging from my stomach to my throat and back. Back and forth and back and forth. My head spun as I tried to balance my steps on the shiny glass floor. The surrounding walls of ruby-flocked wallpaper undulated as I inched my way across the ballroom. I'd become an eight-year-old protagonist in a Grimm's fairy tale, aboard the ocean liner, *Île de France*.

Mummy, at just twenty-seven, looked so beautiful in her navy wool spring coat with matching hat and gloves that I was momentarily distracted from the anguish of her face. How I wished for a last-minute miracle—that she would remain on board when the ship slipped away from its berth.

Passengers gathered along the rails facing the dock. Mummy bent down to hug me, her gray-blue eyes brimming with tears as she turned and headed into the outer corridor. "Dearest, you must try to find Manny," she said, fighting back tears. I had no idea how to find him. All I wanted was to be with her.

The final blast of the ship's horn signaled we were about to leave New York Harbor. Crewmen, stationed by ropes, curled like pythons, were ready to haul them in. Tugboats were positioned to escort us through the harbor, and the final call for loved ones on board sounded. It was time to leave.

My stomach heaved like a heavy surf. I struggled to remain brave as waves of nausea surged, again and again. The ball room was spinning and I wanted to call out, but words were lodged in my throat: *Please don't leave me! Mummy, I need you! I'm so scared! I feel s-o- s-i-c-k...*

Suddenly the room spun even faster; my ears rang and my world went black. With the last wave my stomach emptied... onto the glass floor. A steward in a red-and-black uniform spoke to me, his gentle voice asking, *"Ou sont tes parents?"*

Where were my parents? Can't he see I'm sick? That I'm lost? That I don't know what to do, that I want my mother, that I won't see my mother for over three months! Sois courageux! Ne t'inquietes pas! I must be brave!

The nausea ebbed and I was on more solid footing. *"Je suis avec mon grand-père,"* I answered timidly. *"Maman a dû quitter le navire, et je suis seul parce que je ne peux pas trouver mon grand-père."* He took my hand, saying assuredly, *"Nous allons trouver ton grand-père!"* He finally understood that my mother had had to leave the ship and that I hadn't been able to find my grandfather. He seemed to think my father was nearby: *"Et ton père—ou est- il?"*

"Il est dans le Maine avec mes petites sœurs." While thoughts of my father and sisters at home in Maine made me feel homesick, I liked thinking about them. I was wishing, against all odds, that I might be magically transported back to Maine myself!

Fortunately, Manny had coached me to memorize his cabin number, so I gave the information to the steward.

When I arrived Manny seemed oblivious to my anguish and escorted me to my cabin to take a sponge bath. At that time the protocol for children traveling with someone other than a parent required that they room with people of the same sex. *"Vite! Vite!"* he urged as we were on our way to wave a last goodbye to Mummy. Patience wasn't one of Manny's virtues.

Mummy had found her way to the front row of well-wishers on the dock. She looked ever so distraught when I caught a glimpse of her, searching for us amongst the passengers. I tried to wave but couldn't extend my arm through the tangle of eager adults. The ship's photographer captured Mummy's bewilderment and sadness.

I clung to Manny's hand as we turned and walked together until I felt enough confidence to run ahead. A moment later he called to me: *"Viens vite; il faut voir la Statue de Liberté!"* Together we raced to the deck in time for a viewing of the Statue of Liberty. I held his hand tightly as we joined the crowd assembled along the railing.

"Comme elle est magnifique!" Manny exclaimed as a cigarette smoldered between his lips. "How magnificent she is!" She was, indeed. And enormous! I, on the other hand, was feeling diminutive in size and in confidence. We were leaving New York Harbor, sailing into open water—onto the high seas.

Dinner at the Captain's Table

Four days into our Atlantic crossing, Manny announced that we were invited to be among the guests at the captain's table—that very evening. I was nonchalant. I figured I'd only been invited because I was Manny's "charge." Besides, I wanted to go to Le Guignol puppet show with the other children. Yet I knew how much the invitation meant to Manny and I would not have considered asking to be excused.

"Petit chou, peux-tu me retrouver dans le fumoir après le déjeuner?" He reminded me that events such as this dinner were one of the reasons Rev prepared meals as part of my French lessons—meals that required eating peas without *les petits doigts*, using the right fork or spoon, trying new foods and chewing with my mouth closed. I had a feeling that our meeting to review table manners in the Smoke Room was planned to put me at ease, which would reflect well on both of us.

When I entered the Smoke Room that afternoon, Manny was seated at a wooden table reading a dated newspaper in the dimly lit room, a Gauloises dangling from his lower lip. Smoking was commonplace in the 1950s, so I was surprised to see only three other people in the room: a middle-aged woman with a colorful scarf wrapped stylishly around her head and shoulders, playing solitaire while her cigarette burned to ash in the ashtray. On the other side of the room, two dapper men were wildly gesticulating as they engaged in an animated discussion.

A blue haze rose from Manny's cigarette, drifting toward the ceiling. When I sidled up to him, he reached over and pulled out a chair for me. He explained that together we would review table manners. I curtly replied, *"Je sais tout ça."* I knew how to behave at the table. But when he mentioned that I must try at least one bite of everything on my plate, I overreacted, reminding him of a time, not so long ago, when he insisted I eat a three-minute boiled egg. I hoped to avoid a repeat of that unpleasant event.

Manny obviously wasn't listening as he chain-smoked his unfiltered cigarettes, even smellier than the unfiltered Camels he smoked at home. From past experience I knew belaboring the point would be futile. He went on to tell me what else he expected of me before we went to dinner. In addition to reviewing table manners, he asked me to have a bath and shampoo, followed by clean underwear, my coral-colored dress, white socks and sandals. He, as always, left nothing to chance.

Only then would I be ready for the captain's table.

———————

Due to the ship's policy, I was given a cabin with two older women and they were overly attentive to my needs. They insisted on fussing with my braids, which I'd braided myself before my hair was fully dry. Though still damp, one of the women pinned the braids to the top of my head with a ribbon tied into a bow, something I'd not done before. Just as she was tying the ribbon in place, there was a knock on the cabin door.

I knew right away that it must be Manny, because he always arrived far ahead of schedule when there was a travel deadline. The woman who hadn't been working on my hair answered the door. There stood Manny, glancing into our room as he introduced himself. He looked relieved and pleased to see me in the coral-colored dress.

I looked up at him and said, *"Je dois faire pipi. Je vous retrouverez ici dans deux minutes."* I turned, closing the door before heading to the bathroom.

Manny, meanwhile, waited in the hallway. When I'd finished peeing I looked at myself in the mirror—sideways, then full face. I couldn't resist making facial contortions ending with a smile as I washed and dried my hands. I found Manny waiting impatiently, his hands reaching into his jacket pockets—looking for another cigarette.

Before we left he poked his head in our cabin doorway to thank my cabinmates for being so kind and helpful. *"Charlotte a de la chance d'avoir des compagnons de cabine aussi serviables pour ce voyage."* One of the women clutched her hands together saying that I was *une fille modèle!* Embarrassed by being called a model girl, I grimaced and tugged at Manny's suit jacket, but was relieved to hear such a positive report.

———

The smooth marble floors in the great hallway prompted an irresistible urge to skip, which only frustrated Manny who was trying to point out architectural highlights of the *Île de France*. I was soon short of breath from fiendish skipping. As soon as I stopped to catch my breath, Manny took my hand to calm me down. *"Tu deviens surexcité, ma petite."*

We took our places at the end of a queue that worked its way into the dining room. A young man in a black-and-white uniform greeted us as we entered the room, furnished to accommodate everyone in second class. Each dining table, covered with a white tablecloth and napkins, was set, as it was each evening, with dinnerware, silverware and stemware.

Manny redirected my attention from staring and eavesdropping to helping him find our place cards. Once found, I took my seat beside him. Not seeing any other children, I imagined that they were all at the puppet show and I wished I was there too. Manny, however, was right where he wanted to be and launched into a discussion with the woman on his left.

Glasses clinked, a sign that everyone was to be seated, while the captain stood at the head of the table to welcome guests. As he started to speak I couldn't make out what he was saying, and figured it wasn't of any interest to me anyway. My eye was on the waiter pouring wine into everyone's wine glass. When he came to mine, he grinned then scooped my wine glass off the table. I smiled back as he moved on.

The cheese course arrived on large white platters, balanced by waiters carrying their trays, above their shoulders, on one hand. When a waiter asked me to select some cheeses, I hesitated, trying to figure out which ones smelled so stinky. Manny intervened, asking the waiter to select a small assortment.

As soon as the plate was placed before me I was overcome with a horrible smell. I softly asked Manny to show me which cheese smelled so bad. He pointed out the Limburger and insisted I try a very small bite. I spread the tiniest amount on my bread, took a teensy bite and held the Limburger-laced bread between my teeth, my lips pursed, for as long as I could.

The instant I tried to swallow, that tiny bite shot out of my mouth with a force that surprised no one more than me. Manny thrust out his arm and pointed to the door, ordering me to leave the table. He was not pleased with me and, frankly, I wasn't pleased with him either.

I sheepishly slid out of my chair, pushed it back in and ran head-on into a waiter with a full tray! The sound of crashing dishes and glassware was deafening. Devastated, I avoided looking at anyone, except the waiter. I apologized before bursting into tears as I ran from the dining room.

When I knocked timidly at the door my cabinmates let me in, astonished to see me back so soon. Through racking sobs, I told them what had happened and asked for a glass of ginger ale. It arrived before I'd changed into my pajamas—before they left for dinner.

Manny was aloof for a few days afterwards, but I was used to that. When given a choice between going to bed with ginger ale or dinner at the captain's table, I'd still choose ginger ale every time.

Le Havre to Villeneuve Le Roi

Dawn was breaking when I heard a commotion coming from the corridor and the ship's lights came on signaling our impending arrival in Le Havre. It was 4 a.m., and my cabinmates were already up, finishing packing their suitcases and getting ready for the day ahead. I was hoping to lie on my bunk bed until after they'd left, but they coaxed me into getting up.

The previous evening of merry-making with paper hats and dancing had been great fun. After watching *Annie Get Your Gun*, we got to pick up extra noisemakers and paper decorations, and Jerome even dared me to take sips of abandoned drinks. *"Tu ne dois dire rien à personne!"* I promised I wouldn't tell a soul even though it was mostly melted ice. We made our way to the bar to find Manny who was having a glass of Dubonnet with his Gauloises cigarette.

"Enfin alors! Où étiez -vous depuis le cinéma?"

"Nous nous sommes bien amuser à la fête!" I answered cheerfully.

After telling him about the festive happenings, Manny encouraged Jerome and me to go to our respective rooms to get a good night's sleep. *"Demain, il faut se lever à quatre heures du matin."* He reminded me to have my suitcase all packed before I went to sleep—everything but my nightgown and toothbrush. *"Et n'oublier pas de les mettre dans ta valise demain matin!"*

Jerome was the eldest son of Monsieur and Madame Chambon. I first met him when his family visited Rev and Manny in Kezar Falls. Manny's order to go to bed early was sound. My diary for the next day says "I was well awake."

Manny came to my cabin that morning as he'd agreed to do, and with our suitcases in tow we made our way through the corridors to get in line to disembark. Manny held on to my passport while emphasizing that it mustn't be lost because I would need it as identification wherever we went. Since I had no safe way to hang on to it, Manny kept it in the inside pocket of his suit jacket—alongside his own.

Leaving the ship seemed to take forever, but once on shore we hurried to catch the train to Paris. On this day there would be no two- or three-hour "window" that Manny usually insisted upon. We were to meet Monsieur Tourné at Gare du Nord train station in Paris at a certain time, and there was no way to contact him.

Madame Tourné met us instead since Monsieur Tourné, a pilot, was flying home from Brazzaville in the Congo. Their house in Villeneuve le Roi was close to Orly Airport, about an hour from Paris.

I fell asleep on the ride to Villeneuve le Roi. When Manny reached back and tapped my leg, I couldn't believe we were parked in front of the Tourné's house. Their daughter, Josette, who was my age, greeted me with a large smile and a big bow in her hair. *"Bonjour, Charlotte! Je m'appelle Josette."*

We stood awkwardly beside the car, assessing one another while the grown-ups brought our luggage inside. While Josette and I waited for dinner we jumped rope until she dropped her end of the rope and disappeared into the garage. She came out with her bicycle asking if I wanted to ride.

"*Non, merçi. Je ne sais pas faire du vélo,*" I said, admitting I didn't. I also had to pee so badly I thought my bladder would burst. I had convinced myself that maybe people in France didn't have to pee since no one had mentioned a toilet or a bathroom since we'd arrived. *Wasn't peeing something all mammals did? Why hadn't anyone mentioned this before?* I stood by the house, ashamed that I could no longer hold back and let the warm liquid flow down the insides of my legs, collecting in a puddle around my sandals.

I was embarrassed yet relieved when Madame Tourné finally appeared at the front door to announce dinner was ready. Sheepishly, I mumbled, "*J'ai eu un accident.*" Without over-reacting, she whisked me into the house for a bath and a new change of clothes. When I came back downstairs Josette was helping her grandmother, Madame Fernande, bring the first course to the table.

It wasn't just another meal; it was a feast, beginning with stuffed artichoke. I'd never even seen an artichoke, but that stuffed artichoke was delicious—once Madame Tourné had given me a quick demonstration on how to eat it. She began by pulling a bottom leaf off then she held the top of the leaf and slipped the bottom half into her mouth and slowly pulled the leaf out from her slightly clenched teeth, scraping the pulp from the lower part of the petal. She discarded the petal in a bowl set aside for that purpose. When it was my turn, it felt like all eyes were on me. I pulled a petal from the bottom of my artichoke, held it and slipped the meaty bottom half into my mouth and scraped it with my teeth. *"C'est délicieux!"*

Once the outer and inner petals had been eaten I came to the lavender "choke" which looked silky on the surface, but was fuzzy beneath the petals. Josette showed me how to remove the choke with a spoon to reveal the heart, the best part. Copying Josette, I cut up the heart and dipped each piece into vinaigrette before popping them into my mouth.

When Madame Tourné had cleared the dishes from our first course, Monsieur Tourné stood at the head of the table with a bottle of white wine, offering to refill any empty glasses. Josette and I were titillated when he came to our places and poured a few drops in our water glasses, just as Dad sometimes did at home.

Once we'd finished the main course of roasted chicken with baby potatoes Madame Fernande set a plate of salad greens with vinaigrette at each place. I didn't think I could eat any more, but the servings were small and so delicious. People talked and ate slowly. Josette and I listened to the adult male conversation while Madame Fernande and Madame Tourné were in the kitchen preparing fresh strawberries and cream.

Once the dinner dishes were cleared and washed, Madame Tourné led me to the guest bed in Josette's room. I would be going to school with Josette for the month of June while Manny was in Paris.

Paris and School

Josette and I went with Madame Tourné when she drove Manny to the hotel in Paris where he would be staying to support his "adopted" sons, Hugh Fénier and Phillip Morrell. Their fathers had both been victims of the Nazi holocaust, and Manny provided moral support, guidance and welcomed normalcy. On this trip in addition to outings to the Louvre and a circus, he helped them with their college applications and tuition.

Madame took us to the Jardin d'Acclimatation where we rode a child-size train, swam in the swimming pool, slid down the water slide and fed bread to the pigeons. The next day Madame accompanied Josette and me on our walk to my first day at school, five blocks away.

Although the teacher, Madame Cauvet, was expecting me, Madame Tourné suggested that she introduce us in person, which from my perspective, was reassuring. Right away I noticed that the classroom desks were double-sized, each seating two girls instead of one. My assigned seat was not with Josette, which was probably her mother's doing, since we would have giggled and talked—distracting the other students and each other. Josette was at the top of her class and determined to remain there.

Surprisingly, I kept pace pretty well in all the subjects but math. They were doing long division, and it was not only done very differently, it was far ahead of anything we'd covered at Porter Elementary. On the day of a math exam, Madame Cauvet suggested that, when Josette and I went home for lunch, I stay at home, understanding that I'd probably fail the test, which would be a blow to my self-confidence.

I looked forward to Madame Cauvet's dramatic reading of *Aesop's Fables*, followed by a discussion of the fable's intent. Each student then selected a fable to memorize, in part, and later recite to the class. I chose a French fable by Jean de la Fontaine, "Le Corbeau et le Renard."

All these years later I can still conjure mental images from that poem: A crow holding a cheese in its beak as a fox waits beneath, for the crow to drop the cheese. Having tricked the crow through flattery, the crow opens its beak to sing, dropping the cheese for the fox to claim.

My month with the Tournés ended on a sweet note: returning home from school through a field of scarlet poppies as tall as we were. As we walked Josette took a small tin of raspberry candies from her jacket pocket. We stopped as she handed me a raspberry candy and took one for herself. *"Ne mords pas le bonbon. Suce-le."* We put the candies in our mouths and sucked on them until the centers oozed jelly onto the back of our tongues, ending my stay with Josette on a sweet note, for the next day Manny and I would take the train to Agen, Manny's birthplace. We would spend the next two months living and traveling with Atty, Manny's sister-in-law, in southwestern France.

La Sauvetat

Monsieur Dauphia parked his Peugeot station wagon in front of Atty's house and walked to the front door with his 15-year-old daughter, Odette. Manny greeted them with warm embraces, exclaiming, *"Ça fait trop long- temps!"*

They hadn't seen each other since Manny's last visit in 1945, when WWII ended. I stood on the sidelines until Manny reached out to introduce me. I would return with them to La Sauvetat, an hour south of Agen. I was hesitant, once again, to be leaving for a two-week stay at a farm with people I didn't know, but it turned out to be one of my favorite experiences in France.

Odette and I sat in the back seat of the Peugeot on the drive back to La Sauvetat. Odette, being seven years older, asked me questions about my home, family and school. We forged a common bond when she learned I also lived on a farm with animals and chickens. Her father, Ernest, listened as we talked, occasionally asking questions of his own. I liked Odette and Monsieur Dauphia immediately and realized I was lucky to be going to stay with them.

As Monsieur Dauphia drove to the front of their farmhouse, a flock of geese lifted their wings, and darted, helter-skelter, across the yard, honking noisily while chickens continued to scratch for grain and insects. Odette had cautioned me about their combative geese, so we waited until they were at a safe distance before getting out of the car.

Monsieur Dauphia ignored the geese and went to greet his neighbors who were helping him with his wheat harvest. The helpers were seated at a long table in the shade of the overhang at the side of the farmhouse. They devoured Madame Dauphia's hearty *soupe au pistou* with vegetables, herbs and lots of garlic. The table was spread with loaves of crusty bread taller than I was, bowls of farmer cheese, pitchers of well water and bottles of red wine. Since La Sauvetat operated as a communal village where neighbors helped one another, Madame Dauphia fulfilled her role by preparing hearty, delicious meals for the ravenous farmhands. This procedure repeated until all communal members harvested all of their wheat.

I followed Odette across the yard like a well-trained dog, staying out of her way while awed by her imposing presence. She moved her sturdy frame intentionally and with seeming ease. She rarely looked at me when she spoke. Her thick, ebony-colored hair, pulled back with a headband, rested on her shoulders. Like her mother, she wore either dresses or skirts with frilly blouses, covered by a house-coat type apron and sensible shoes.

The remaining soup still simmered in a large ceramic pot. The aroma was so tantalizing I asked Odette if we could have some. She motioned to me to follow her onto the patio where Madame Dauphia had left two bowls of hot soup. A few flies discovered it before we had, but that didn't deter either of us. *"C'est pour nous—de la soupe?"* I asked.

"Mais certainement!" Odette replied. From the first spoonful I knew that I was eating something I would never forget. Madame Dauphia's *soupe au pistou* has remained

a lifelong favorite.

After we finished our soup and the farmhands returned to the wheat field, Odette asked if I wanted to watch the ceremony that signaled the end of the Dauphia's harvest. Having no idea what she was referring to, I shrugged and replied with indifference, *"Bien sûr."*

It was hot in the sun, and I had dressed with shorts, T-shirt and sandals to walk on the wheat stubble. In the field the farmhands had built a traditional, life-size, *maison de paille*. Traditionally, someone special places a vase of flowers at the peak of the straw house. Monsieur Dauphia asked if I would climb the ladder and leave the flowers this year. Odette offered to climb partway up the ladder with the vase. All I had to do was reach down and bring the vase to its resting place. Cheers broke out as I made a secure place for the vase and its flowers. With the vase left atop the house, the ceremony was complete and I descended the ladder.

Looking up at the flowers against the azure sky I felt like a character from a fairy tale.

Surveying Land By Oxen Cart

"Eh la, Charlotte, il faut que tu te lèves tout de suite. Ernest va partir pour les champs en quinze minutes!"

Madame Dauphia woke me up before dawn, before the Toulouse geese honked from their pen; before the giant-sized loaves of bread were delivered, even before the cliff swallows searched for winged insects to feed their young.

Monsieur Dauphia was headed out to survey the wheat crop across the open expanse of fields at La Sauvetat. When he had asked me if I'd like to go with him by ox cart, he couldn't miss the excitement of the grin spread across my face. My wish had been granted: I wouldn't have to go to the outdoor market with Odette and her mother who talked mostly to each other about things I didn't understand or care about. They were almost like sisters and even looked alike! I didn't like feeling like an outsider—which I, of course, was.

I hastily put on my underwear, shorts and a T-shirt. I raced to the primitive pit latrine in the cow shed at the bottom of the knoll. Before I raised the wooden latch of the shed door, I made sure I was alone, then hurriedly stepped inside and planted my feet on the worn wooden foot holders on either side of the open pit. I scooched down, holding my underwear and shorts from behind while avoiding looking or falling into the murky waste below.

In no time I pulled up my shorts and hurried outside as fast as I could go.

That outhouse gave me the creeps with its overpowering stench and ropes of cobwebs. It was also at least fifty yards from the house, a considerable distance when one needed "to go" in a hurry!

I tucked in my shirt as I ran. Monsieur Dauphia, his wooden cattle stick in hand, waited for me as I reached the top of the knoll. Stained, white oxen shifted their bulky bodies, swishing their tails in continuous motion, waiting for their command to move ahead. Monsieur extended his hand to assist, as I climbed into the wooden cart. With my arms outstretched for balance, I walked to the back of the tilted cart and dangled my legs over the edge.

"*Allons,*" Monsieur Dauphia directed as he raised his long stick. Creaking and moaning the cart lurched into the rutted path behind the oxen. The Dauphia farm faded from view as we trekked the ancient route. The sun lit the eastern sky while a steady breeze blew from across the prairie. As far as I could see, yellow ochre waves of wheat thrummed against the azure sky. *Je n'oublirai jamai cette paysage.* I have never forgotten that landscape and its magnificence, a spiritual experience.

As the cart reached the brow of a small incline, Monsieur abruptly brought it to a standstill though it seemed an unlikely place to stop. We hadn't even reached a plateau. The oxen, heads lowered under the weight of the yoke, shifted from side to side, flicking their tails to ward off the swarming flies. Monsieur Dauphia suggested I go behind a nearby shrub if I needed to *faire pee pee.* He, momentarily, disappeared to do the same.

It was already mid-morning, and we still had farther to

go. When he reappeared, Monsieur used the palm of his hand to draw an imaginary map of the land, showing me where we were in relation to La Sauvetat. Unbeknownst to me, we had traveled a circular route that would eventually lead back home. Before climbing on the cart Monsieur reached into his jacket pocket and pulled out a paper satchel with two hunks of bread, two hunks of cheese and a cucumber, split in half. We quenched our thirst with water from a flask, ate the bread and cheese then continued on our way.

I was loving this adventure as I took my place at the back of the cart, feeling a renewed sense of self-confidence. I looked back at Monsieur just as he raised his stick and commanded, *Allons!* We were off again as the oxen plodded ahead, the wooden cart groaning and creaking behind them.

The sun was hot. I pulled my shirt over the back of my head for protection, my arms still in sleeves. Orphaned clouds provided a temporary relief from the scorching sun.

Again, Monsieur Dauphia ordered the oxen to halt. He rose from his seat, climbed down from the cart, and walked past the oxen to a smallish quivering mound of feathers between the dried ruts. The mound moved! Gingerly he picked the bird up in his *mouchoir*, the handkerchief he kept in the breast pocket of his jacket. He walked toward me with his hands outstretched. *"Peut-tu tenir l'oiseau dans tes mains?"*

"Mais, oui!" Enthusiastically, I held my hands out as Monsieur transferred the bird, a swallow of some kind, to me to hold. I pushed up against the side of the cart, hoping for more support as I tried to maintain a gentle but firm hold on the injured bird. Monsieur gave me a nod I

interpreted as approval then returned to his seat. *"Allons!"*

A raptor circled and I held the bird even closer to my chest. As it grew increasingly hot I tried to provide shade for the little bird. We seemed to have been heading into the sun ever since it rose that morning. It was now high overhead as we made the last leg of our trek. *"Mon petit oiseau, tu va survivre,"* I said softly. The swallow's eye lids were lowered, occasionally blinking, but mostly they were shut as I repeatedly ran my index finger front to back across the top of its wee head. I lowered my head and again whispered, *"Tu va survivre."* The swallow opened its beak, wide. *What if its mother is looking for it? What should I feed it? I wish we could move a little faster!*

At the far end of the horizon I saw the Dauphia farm. We'd be there in time for soup at the long table beneath the grape arbor—that is, if Madame and Odette were back from marketing. When the oxen finally stopped in front of the Dauphia's barn, I was anxious to jump out and care for the swallow; but first I had to make a nest. *"Monsieur, je veux faire un nid pour l'oiseau,"* I said. *"Puis-je laissez le dans le chariot pour quelques minutes?"*

Monsieur agreed that I could leave the swallow for a few minutes while he watered the oxen at the stone water trough. *"Soit vite!"* he urged.

I scooped up some straw and small feathers. *Perfect!* Now I only needed to add water to some dried mud in order to hold the nest together. I called out to Monsieur, *"Ou puis-je trouver un bidon? J'ai besoin de l'eau pour faire du boue."* Monsieur directed me to the barn. *"Merci!"* I shouted, racing toward the barn.

The cans were on the shelf by the grain bins but I couldn't reach them without a stool, even standing on tip-toes. So I looked around for something else. *I have to hurry!* I noticed, in a far back corner, the remains of a chair, now just a seat and legs where Monsieur sat while he shelled beans in the shade.

I was lifting the semi-chair when Monsieur appeared at the front of the barn. *"Charlotte, l'hirondelle n'est plus dans le chariot! Peut-être qu'elle a voler!"*

The swallow had flown away. Even though it had been too sick to fully open its eyes such a short time ago, I was relieved to know that my little charge had recovered. I returned to the front of the barn, and Monsieur and I stood together in the wide doorway, hoping for a one last glimpse of the swallow.

Les Eyzies

It was still early-morning when we stepped off the train at Gare des Eyzies from Paris. Manny and I spent most of the day at the prehistoric caves of Les Eyzies, settled more than 460,000 years ago. The cave dwellers had an eye for beauty as evidenced by the paintings on the cave walls in the Dordogne region.

Before we began our tour of the caves we decided to have breakfast at a nearby café—just steps from the train station. Manny ordered coffee for himself and a *café au lait* for me, and a croissant for each of us. As we ate he gave me a simplified history of what I was about to see when we entered the caves.

No amount of preparation could have prepared me for what I was about to see! For the first time in weeks, Manny gave me his undivided attention as we explored these cave paintings of bison and the older artifacts carved from tusks of mammoths. The bison, painted so confidently, were captured in a few simple strokes, and the needles carved from bone or ivory delighted me most of all. They were beautifully made with tools fashioned from stone.

When we entered a room with "squeletons" (as noted in my diary) of a woman and a bear I initially found them creepy until we spent more time looking at them. I had never seen a human skeleton, and my diary indicates that the woman's skeleton resembled a monkey, and the bear's head looked like a moose. Mammoth teeth were "big like my head because the mammoth was nearly two times the size of an elephant."

It was late afternoon when we emerged from the cave. After a wonderful dinner in Les Eyzies Manny and I took the train home to Agen where Atty was waiting.

Olga

Diary entry, Tuesday, June 20, 1950:
I am at the real country now. I am going to feed the
chickens, cows, rabbits, hens and the pigs...

An older man with a shock of white hair met us at the station platform. Manny and I drove with him to his farm where we met his wife, his daughter Olga and her toddler, Pierrot, dressed in a woolen sunsuit the color of turmeric. Olga, a lovely twenty-something, had a sunny disposition, a genuine smile and took an interest in everything around her. Like my mother, she pointed out details in nature: birds' nests; patterns on butterfly wings and flower petals; cloud formations; and the sweet fragrance of *muguet* (lily of the valley) that grew on the shady side of their farm.

Olga was born in Russia and fled to France with her parents in 1940 when Hitler was hell-bent on wiping out Russians and starving hundreds of thousands of them to death. Nine years later Pierrot was born.

Unlike other people I met in France, Olga asked me what I enjoyed doing. It took me but a second to tell her that I liked helping with chores, especially outdoor chores. Knowing this she asked me to help her feed the pigs, chickens, cows and rabbits. When she asked if I'd watch Pierrot while she fed the baby chicks, I was overjoyed.

Instead of feeling that I was in the way, I finally felt useful and included while Manny attended to his affairs elsewhere.

Olga invited Alette, her neighbor, to spend the next day with us. Olga thought I'd enjoy playing with someone my own age—a reasonable assumption. In fact, I was perfectly content to be with just Olga. I felt needed as I filled grain cans, scattered grain for the hens and held Pierrot's hand to distract him while Olga milked the two cows.

The following day Alette arrived mid-morning to spend the day. We played tag until Alette had another idea. She asked if I liked rolling *les cerceaux.* I told her that I'd only seen photos of children rolling hoops in Paris, but I'd like to try.

"Très bien, alors," Alette said, on her way to the clothesline. Olga, by this time, was hanging out the wash, and Alette asked if she and I could go to her house to get two hoops. Olga shook out the wet shirt, hesitating long enough to say, *"Bien sûr! C'est une bonne idée, Alette!"*

Alette's house was less than ten minutes away. When we got there she went straight to the shed where the hoops hung on a wooden peg. *"Maintenant, je vais te montrer comment on fait rouler un cerceau,"* she said as she lifted them carefully from the peg. *"C'est plus difficile qu'il apparaît."*

When she handed me the smooth wooden hoop, I was surprised to find that it came up to my waist! Alette showed me how to push the hoop from just behind the top to keep it rolling. Their bumpy driveway didn't help, but after a series of tries I finally got the hoop to stay up and roll ahead. Alette was right; it was way more difficult to keep the hoop rolling than it appeared. We rolled them back to Olga's and played near the barn where the ground was smooth. It wasn't until Olga called us to come in for lunch that we knew we'd lost track of time. After washing our hands at the kitchen sink we sat down to a simple meal of French bread, salami and cucumber slices.

We'd been actively playing for over two hours, so after lunch, while Pierrot was having his nap, Olga's mother asked Alette to play checkers, giving me a welcome moment of solitude. Olga, meanwhile, beckoned me to an outbuilding where she kept her bicycle. It looked twice as large as Josette's in Villeneuve le Roi.

Determined to learn to ride on my own, I tried and tried. Olga helped me, even though I couldn't sit on the seat and touch the pedals. I tried balancing, standing on the pedals while she stood beside me, holding me upright until the bicycle wobbled and fell over. We repeated this process over and over. Olga managed to keep me from getting hurt and the bike from getting dented by grabbing the handle bars just before they hit the ground. I was too small, but Olga encouraged me nonetheless. Unlike Manny, Olga didn't lose her patience.

Alette came out in time to watch me tip over one more time. She was on her way home; and I was sorry to see her go but distracted in my determination to ride a bike. Olga had been right: I did enjoy playing with someone my own age, in spite of my initial hesitation. Saying goodbye was awkward for both of us. Alette put the hoops over her arm as she left.

"*Au revoir,*" I said wistfully.

After this very full day, Manny had returned from wherever he'd been, and we all sat down for a family dinner of homemade borscht followed by roasted chicken and a green salad. Everything we ate came from their farm—except the wine, of which I had just a teaspoon, added to my water. When dinner was over, Olga saw that I was too tired to help clear the table so she asked me to say *bonsoir* to everyone before taking me to my room. She made sure I washed, brushed my teeth and went *pipi* before getting into bed.

In less than five minutes I was sound asleep.

———————

Rain, splattering on the window panes, awakened me from a deep sleep the next morning. As I pulled back the curtains, rain droplets were popping up like hailstones, hitting the roof tiles with a satisfying sound.

I loved rainy days wherever I was, but especially at home. *Were my sisters playing house with their dolls as they often did when it rained?* I missed being there when Mummy set up the easel (in the basement) for us to paint. Or when she let me go to my room to read the latest Nancy Drew mystery. *But I mustn't be thinking of home! I'm a long way from home—all the way across the Atlantic Ocean.*

Olga reminded me the night before to pack my bag, except for the clothes I'd be wearing. I put on my sundress and packed my T-shirt and shorts, along with my diary, in my overnight bag.

Manny was at the table entertaining Pierrot when I came downstairs. *"Bonjour"* I said, giving Manny a kiss on his cheek. In the kitchen Olga was preparing for our *petit déjeuner* of *café au lait* and *pain au chocolat*. I was sad to leave.

Once the breakfast dishes had been washed, Olga left

Pierrot with her parents and drove us to the train station so we could catch the noon train back to Agen. I'd been with Olga only a few days, but she sensed my sorrow at the prospect of leaving. She parked along the entrance to the train station and Manny opened the back door so I could climb out. Olga quietly came around to my side of the car and placed her arm around my shoulder. *"Charlotte, J'ai quelque chose pour toi,"* she said as she handed me a yellow calico bag with orange and blue flowers.

"Puis-je regarder dedans?" I asked excitedly.

Olga beamed. *"Mais certainement; c'est pour toi!"*

I untied the ribbon and placed my hand in the bag. I felt... a head... body... legs... and arms while I slowly lifted the wooden doll from the bag she'd made. I couldn't suppress my excitement. *"Et comment s'appelle t'elle?"*

"Elle s'appelle Aline!" she said. *"Elle était ma poupée préférée quand j'avais huit ans."* Olga was giving me her favorite doll! I clutched Aline close to my chest; unable to contain my joy, I ran around to the other side of the car where Manny was smoking, keeping an anxious eye on the station. I held Aline up for him to see. *"Olga me l'a donner,"* I said excitedly.

Manny's response, while consistent, was crushing. *"Tu n'as pas besoin d'une poupée! Rends-la à Olga, tout de suite!"* An instant pall was cast over my short-lived thrill. My eyes welled with tears as I reluctantly shuffled back to Olga holding Aline in my out-stretched hands. I explained, between sobs, that Manny said I must return her—that I didn't need a doll.

Olga hugged me tightly as I handed Aline back. She understood my great disappointment. She also knew Manny and understood his insistence. My heart was hollowed out by Manny's inability to understand that my disappointment wasn't about the doll per se. Yes, I had a doll at home, and I didn't even care that much about dolls. Rather, it was that Olga had given me her precious doll. That's what meant the world to me.

Before leaving, Olga hugged me tight, and my eyes welled with tears. I was heartbroken. I missed my mother. And I already missed Olga.

———

I followed Manny into the train station lugging my overnight bag. Since we had round-trip tickets to Agen he needed only a daily newspaper to pass the time. When Manny offered to take my bag I eagerly left it and set off exploring the doorways of narrow stuccoed buildings outside the train station.

The direct sun was just too hot. I was so thirsty I could think of nothing but getting something to drink. The fancy gold lettering of BAR caught my eye on the large-shop window. I peered inside, but it was so dark my eyes needed a few seconds to adjust—to notice a man bent over a billiard table with his cue stick on a ball. I watched. Nothing happened.

He stood upright and rubbed the end of his cue with something in his hand. I was way too thirsty to keep watching. Instead, I walked back to the station where Manny was still reading the newspaper. *"J'ai tellement soif, et il y a un bar juste à côté d'ici,"* I said when he glanced up. *"Pouvons-nous cherchez quelques chose à boire?"*

Instead of asking me to wait, Manny stood up, folded his paper and tucked it in his sports jacket pocket. He followed me to the bar next door and held the door as we walked inside to instant relief! An overhead fan whirred, moving the sultry air just enough for me to shiver.

"Petit bonhomme, qu'est-ce que tu veux boire?" Manny asked. *"Une limonade?"*

Mais oui, j'aimerai beaucoup une limonade!" I could have drunk two, possibly three lemonades, but I'd happily start with one. Manny ordered a *café au lait*, and we seated ourselves at a small table where I could keep my eye on the billiard player who appeared annoyed as he lay his cue on the table with a shrug of his shoulders. He was leaving!

After the man left, Manny finished his coffee and walked with me to the long green table to show me how to hold the cue stick so I could "practice" playing billiards. I loved the colorful, shiny balls and the click they made when they collided.

For the first time, I wished Manny had gotten someplace even earlier.

Basque Country

It was in the first week of June when Manny, Atty and I left on a trip to the Basque country in southwestern France. Atty's neighbors drove us first to the medieval city of Carcassonne in the Languedoc, and from there we went on to Saint-Jean-de-Luz and Biarritz, where I romped on the beach and found a dried-out seahorse amongst a pile of debris. The seahorse was about three inches long, perfectly intact and would be an exceptional addition to my growing collection of natural objects. I wrapped it in a handkerchief and put it in my suitcase pocket along with a few seashells and other treasures.

From Biarritz we traveled to Bayonne, then on to Saint-Jean-Pied-de-Port, a small town on the Spanish border where clouds hung like heavy gray blankets, keeping it from being unbearably hot. I was itching to get out and run around when our driver parked in the lot at the Spanish border. Manny explained that as I looked out the car window I was looking into Spain—that the uniformed guards who patrolled back and forth, with their rifles swinging from their backs, were there to maintain order. With lips pursed they looked grim, not showing even a hint of a smile. *If I jumped over the border, clearly defined by a white line painted across the roadway, I could say I'd been to Spain!*

I kept my eyes peeled on the guards while Manny and the driver stood smoking and talking beside the car. Atty was fast asleep in the car. Trying not to attract attention I skipped back and forth, inching my way ever closer to the border, waiting for the guards to become distracted. It finally happened when a car with a hole in its muffler came speeding toward the border from Spain. While no one was watching I seized the moment and jumped with both feet, in and out of Spain, and ran back to the parking lot.

Manny, who had been watching, was not amused. I, on the other hand, was titillated by accomplishing something forbidden yet seemingly harmless. No one had been hurt in any way, and I had accomplished my mission. I assured Manny that the guards had not noticed; but Manny reminded me that my childish prank could have led to a sinister outcome under Spain's dictator, Francisco Franco.

———————

Behind us, like a jagged wall were the snow-covered Pyrenees which we would explore on our way back. We spent the night in a cozy mountainside hotel, in the heart of the mountains. Manny shared a room with the driver, and I shared a room with Atty. Sunlight streamed through the window waking us early on the following day, but it wasn't hot, so we took a small train to the summit of the closest mountain where I walked on a glacier over two hundred meters deep while Manny, Atty and the driver stood along the roadside, talking. The sunlight reflecting off the glacier was so blinding I had to squint. Nothing but space, the glacier and expansive blue sky as far as I could see. That evening we attended a Basque pelota championship where men in white shirts and shorts hit the ball over a net and against a wall with basket-shaped rackets attached to their hands. The sound made by the ball hitting the wall was really loud, like a bullet striking a stationary object. I was caught up in the excitement and I even nicknamed one player Friser (pronounced Free-zay) for his head of thick black curls. Friser just happened to be one of the star players of the game.

Our final stop was Lourdes, a concession to Atty, who had personal reasons for wanting to visit the Massabielle Grotto, a top destination for Roman Catholics. From the moment we arrived until we left I was repelled, out of my element and downright miserable. It wasn't that I didn't have empathy for people with infirmities, but I'd never been surrounded by a sea of grim faces, all dressed in somber blacks and grays, praying as they leaned on their crutches. I felt light-headed. Atty must have noticed that I was dehydrated and pale because a short time later she handed me a paper cup with holy water from the grotto. Being thirsty I drank it, and felt only slightly better. *So much for the holy water.* Atty pointed out a parade of weak, sickly and lame people moving by on their crutches toward the grotto where they drank holy water. When they marched back, they were without their crutches. Atty called it a miracle. I was skeptical then and even more so now.

Seeing a girl about my age with leg braces and crutches upset me so I turned to ask Atty if she would ever be able to walk again, only Atty was nowhere in sight; nor was Manny. I was momentarily terrified, but remembered that Manny had told me to always stay where I was if I ever got separated from him. Eventually Manny saw me and raised his arm to attract my attention. I burst into tears and wanted to leave. That had been the last straw.

We made our way back to the car and drove away as the wall of crutches receded behind us.

Manny, Atty and Charlotte

Final Days in Paris

Excerpts from my diary suggest that by mid-August I was ready to return home—and that Manny was ready for me to return home, as well: "I did so much showing off I was sent to bed early. This gave a lesson to the others."

Two days after my visit to the farmers market in Agen, I left on a five-hour train trip to Paris with Manny and Atty. They sat together, and I sat opposite them, next to the window. I played a game with Atty, finding things in the landscape that began with each letter of the alphabet. It wasn't long before I saw cattle grazing and said enthusiastically, *animaux!* Time passed quickly, and Atty seemed to enjoy the game as well. Manny was distracted, reading the newspaper he had tucked into his suit coat pocket.

When he finished with the newspaper, Manny folded it neatly and laid it on the seat beside him. *"Mon petit choux, est-ce que tu as faim?"* I had been so busy finding things in the landscape that I hadn't thought about lunch, but once brought to my attention I was ready. Atty had packed our lunch in a cloth sack with three napkins. Atty handed me a napkin to spread out on my lap followed by my baguette with saucisson and two fresh apricots. Being thirsty the apricots tasted especially delicious and helped quench my thirst.

While we ate, a sturdily-built middle-aged woman entered our compartment and sat close to the doorway. She had boarded at the last stop and didn't look at us when she sat down. I was watching her when I caught her glance sideways at us before bringing her sandwich out of her bag. Manny spoke to her, but she didn't respond. She hadn't realized he was speaking to her until she saw that he was looking at her with his mouth moving. She brought her hands to her ears and shook her head, signaling that she was deaf. She finished eating her sandwich, closed her eyes and soon her head slumped to one side with her lower lip drooped.

The woman woke up shortly before the train came to a stop at Montparnasse. We had arrived at our destination and the three of us got off the train with our baggage while the lady continued to sit.

Gie and Élianne, a young couple whose engagement party we had attended, met us at the train station to ferry us to Madame Boularan's home at 12 Rue Lecuirot in Paris. With Élianne snuggled close beside him, Gie drove through the maze of narrow streets like a cheetah going after its prey, until Manny asked him to slow down. *"Tu vas si vite que je ne vois pas où nous sommes."* Manny was afraid that, at the speed we were going, he wouldn't recognize Madame Boularan's house; Gie depended on Manny's directions to get us to our destination.

Madame Boularan had invited Manny and me to spend our last few days in France with her on the final leg of our three-and-a-half-month journey. Atty stayed at Madame Boularan's as well.

Her backyard was a Parisian oasis of fruit trees: cherry, plum, apple and pear; an herb garden; flower beds; and linden and chestnut trees. Coco, her African gray parrot, sat in his cage in the shade in that oasis when it wasn't raining. To make sure the cage remained in the shade, Madame Boularan asked me to tell her when the cage needed to be moved. I liked helping and alerted her as soon as a glimmer of sunlight reached Coco's cage.

When I asked Coco "*répéter après moi,* Polly wants a cracker," he didn't respond. It dawned on me that he might only speak French so I taught him a new phrase: *Coco est joli,* wishfully thinking that flattery would get him to drop one of his scarlet tail feathers which would have made a colorful addition to my feather collection. It didn't happen.

It poured rain on our last day in Paris. Being aware that I needed to stay occupied, Madame Boularan asked if there was something I would like to make. I knew right away I'd like to make a stuffed cat for Atty, so Madame Boularan gave me a piece of paper and pencil to make my pattern. She let me choose my fabric from a basket of remnants and gave me a needle and thread. I chose a swatch of teal flannel with abstract touches of red and green. She reminded me to leave a space open to add the cotton stuffing since I was stitching so quickly. It was the perfect project for my last day in Paris, and Atty actually knew that it was supposed to represent a cat!

Manny's friend George brought us to the Gare Saint Lazare to catch the train to Le Havre where we would board the *Île de France.* In my diary I wrote that "poor Atty" came with us but left in tears with George when we got on the train. She would be taking a train back to Agen alone.

On the train I wrote in my diary: *We saw houses that where (sic) struck down and . . . fences that were all struck by the Germans.*

The visible scars of WWII were grim reminders of war. Manny made certain I saw the effects of war on people, villages and especially children. He succeeded. I've never forgotten.

———

Transitions are challenging, and returning home was no exception. Having a week aboard the *Île de France* gave me a chance to decompress; but it also gave me time to grow anxious, wondering if I would still be a part of our family. *Would my friends still accept me?* I knew I'd had experiences none of my classmates had had, that I had changed in some ways. I had also missed out on experiences they had had. *Would my family and friends know that I was the same person?*

In looking back on my journey with Manny, my recollections of the transatlantic voyage to France are vivid, while memories of the return trip are almost non-existent. My diary entries on the return trip are scant, revealing only my pleasure in having Jerome to play with and watching for flying fish.

Meeting Mummy at the dock is my most vivid memory of the return trip. I flew into her arms and burst into tears.

The Blue Goose

It was mid-July and seasonably warm when Daddy put up a second swing in the maple trees as Kathy and I were eager to swing together—on our own swings. Attached to high branches the thick, long ropes pushed through holes on either side of the wooden plank seats, and double-knotted on the underside.

Louise, still too small to swing, sat on the edge of the nearby hammock with her wooly pony grasped in one hand. She watched as I helped Kathy settle into the middle of her seat while reaching out for my swing. Standing on my tip-toes I wiggled onto the plank, then pumped as hard and as fast as I could until I was swinging as high as I could go, shrieking with excitement.

"I can go higher than you can!" I shouted as I pumped until the swing was almost parallel to the branch it was attached to. "I can go higher!" Kathy shouted back.

Meanwhile Rev walked up the path to our house to ask Mummy about a ride to town to pick up "provisions" from Kelly's Market. Rev noticed us swinging and exclaimed nostalgically, "Oh, to be a little girl again!" She sounded so envious that I stopped pumping, and slowly brought my swing to a standstill.

"Revy! You wanna try swinging?" I asked, jumping off and holding the seat high to see. Without hesitation she walked toward my swing carefully avoiding getting in Kathy's way. Holding onto the rope I jumped off the swing and watched Rev as she settled onto the seat, tucked her dress beneath her to keep it from flying up and leaned back. She stuck one leg out in front of the other and pushed the ground with her back foot. She moved slowly forward, then back in a slow, steady rhythm.

"Revy, go higher!" Kathy urged. Rev wrapped her arms around the ropes so they were in the crooks in her arms. "Pump, Revy!" I urged, as she moved like a pendulum on a grandfather clock: forward, back, forward... pushing but never going much higher. "Rev, see how high I can go!" Kathy shouted, while she pumped higher and higher.

Mummy stepped out to join us, surprised to see Rev swinging. "Well, it appears that everyone is getting into the act!" Mummy said casually. "I'd forgotten to tell you, Revy, that Nardo and I have a chance to see *A Moon for the Misbegotten*. The O'Neill play. It's at The Barnstormers, only thirty minutes away." Rev continued to sit on her swing, though it had stopped.

"What a marvelous opportunity, Alse. And, I must add, a happy coincidence. If Manny feels up to it we'll ask the girls to spend the night."

————

After a supper of fresh asparagus and cheese omelet and my favorite dessert, lemon sponge pudding, Grammy cleared the table of dishes while I filled the dish pan a third full with water. It was my turn to wash dishes and Kathy's turn to dry. Daddy went to the living room to read the newspaper while Mummy helped Gram put dry dishes away.

For me, an adventure could begin and end close to home: an overnight with Rev and Manny. Our overnight bags were packed with a toothbrush, pajamas, clean change of clothes and a stuffed animal or favorite doll. I packed Blue, my faded velveteen rabbit, whose long ears had been stiffened with copper wire stitched along their edges by Manny, who was compelled to keep things in good repair. Kathy tucked Raggedy Ann into her bag, and Louise had her wooly pony nestled in the crook of her arm.

We kissed our parents goodnight and walked, single file, along the path through the pine plantation. It had been several weeks since Kathy and Louise had been to the Raffy's. I wondered if this was because of the blue goose Manny said he kept in the north room. Manny never failed to mention the blue goose when Louise and Kathy visited, probably because Louise invariably stuck her thumb in her mouth, forgetting the consequences. My sisters were understandably afraid of this goose. While I wanted to believe it was a fabrication, I wasn't entirely sure either.

My sisters and I walked along the path of burnt-orange pine needles strewn with twigs, emerging from the woods into the Raffy's field. As we approached the house, Kathy stopped abruptly, moving closer to me, "What's that scary noise?"

The peepers' high trill was almost deafening. "Those are peepers!"

"I know what peepers sound like! There!! I just heard it again. Did you hear that?" I had heard it.

"That's a fox, probably a mother, hunting for field mice to feed her kits." Louise grabbed Kathy's hand.

I walked ahead, listening to my sisters behind me.

"Will the blue goose be there tonight?" Louise asked.

"I hope not!" said Kathy.

"What if I suck my thumb while I'm asleep?"

"Louise, don't suck your thumb!" Kathy urged. "Put your hand under the pillow where you can't reach it."

I joined in as they caught up with me. "If there is a blue goose, it won't be able to get out of the north room because the door is latched."

Silence.

We followed the trodden path to the Raffy's front door. I knocked on the dark green, wood-paneled door, and seconds later we were greeted by Rev. "Come in, girls. *Charlotte, tu peux porter les valises en haut.*"

Why can't she just ask me to bring the bags upstairs in English, so I don't feel so awkward and my sisters can understand what she's saying? However, I'd learned not to quibble with Rev—ever!

I made three trips up the steep stairs, each trip ending with a bag beside a bed. In the meantime, my sisters gingerly patted Gambo, the Newfoundland whose smell was highly offensive to all but Rev. He welcomed their attention sprawled on the living room floor with strings of drool seeping from his drooping jowls. He raised and lowered his tail, making a series of wapping sounds when he wanted the attention of anyone entering the room.

Journey's End was a repository for paper of all sorts. As a devoted reader of *The New York Times*, Rev was forever clipping articles to slip inside a relevant book or send to her many correspondents, most of whom had musical or literary connections like Leonard Bernstein, Henry Beston and Willa Cather.

There were numerous tables and chairs, and an upright Baldwin piano with a bench that held scores of sheet music by Jerome Kern, Irving Berlin and the Gershwins, in addition to original sheet music by her father, Arthur Foote. Since Rev was an only child, she inherited her father's estate—but donated the bulk of it to charitable causes like Morgan Memorial, Boston Conservatory of Music and Williams College. Countless framed photos of family and friends cluttered their small living room along with their Silvertone radio, cased in wood; a heavy wooden desk with carved-angel drawer pulls; and red geraniums blooming on the south-facing window sills.

Since Manny avoided wasting anything, he used the basswood, blown down on their property in the hurricane of 1938, instead of pine to panel the entire downstairs. It was clear and without knots! He even paneled above the fireplace, a major source of heat in the wintertime.

Chimney swifts built their nests of twigs and raised their young on the brick ledges inside that same chimney in the summertime. I loved hearing the whooshing air as they dove into their cavernous, creosote-encrusted home to feed their chirping chicks the flying insects they'd caught mid-air.

———

The second floor of Rev's was akin to being transported on a magic carpet to a faraway place. The floors were of southern pine, adorned with white, loosely felted rugs of goat hair colorfully embroidered with turquoise and deep yellow-orange designs. They originated in the Middle East or, more likely, in Turkey where Rev and Manny lived for two years after they'd married. My sisters stayed in the bedroom facing west, the brighter of the two rooms. It had two matching twin beds painted in ivory enamel. Rev painted everything needing paint either ivory, oak or dark green enamel.

My appropriated bedroom faced east and had a three-quarter iron bed (ivory enamel) and a small plastered fireplace whose damper was kept shut to keep rain and chimney swifts out. Like most early New England farmhouses, there were no closets. Rather, each bedroom had a garret with built-in shelves for clothing and other belongings. Rev's long-haired cat, Ginger, found these shelves an ideal sleeping place, as well as easy access to unsuspecting mice scampering in via the hole once gnawed in the garret wall.

The beds were made with linen sheets and pillowcases that covered horsehair pillows and mattresses. Each bed had a woolen blanket and printed cotton bedspread from India. At the end of the hall was the guest room where Louise and Kathy laid wooly pony and Raggedy Ann on their respective beds before going to the windows to look out into the field and hillside beyond the woods. I heard them coming across their room and through the hallway.

"Can we see the little man who does somersaults?" Kathy asked as she and Louise stood beside the trunk filled with treasure.

"Good idea! I'll open the trunk, but you two stand back so the cover won't hit you when I pull it up." I turned the iron skeleton key that Rev kept in the lock then slipped my left hand into the carved handle insert and pulled up, while holding up the cover. The smell of old books, lavender, washing soap and dry wood pervaded the air and drew us into another time. We all peered into the trunk.

Lying on top was a French celluloid flute. I blew a few shrill notes then placed it on my bed, along with postcards from Turkey in a brittle envelope covered with fancy canceled stamps. I carefully moved the sword to one side of the trunk; it was wrapped in light corrugated cardboard with blood still visible on the blade.

Kathy picked out the large seed pod from Martinique and shook it, rattling the seeds inside for a rich, mellow sound. She shook, half-heartedly, as I reached for the hand-sewn, cotton bag containing the little three-inch man. "Look who I found!" I exclaimed as I gently pulled out the little man.

His two-dimensional body of silk was glued to a cardboard cylinder head with finely drawn facial features in sepia ink, defining his cheerful character. A yellow plastic cap, glued on top, kept the lead weight inside the cylinder from falling out.

"Louise, will you hold him while I look for something we can use for a hill for him to somersault on?"

I stooped to enter the garret and looked around. *Perfect!* There, right in front of me, on the top shelf resting on two, inch-squared, rectangular wooden prisms. It was about eighteen inches long, an inch thick and eight inches wide. I lifted the board off the prisms and set it up in the bedroom so one end lay on the bottom rung of a straight-backed ladder chair. I then lifted the bottom of the board up to make it parallel with the rung of the chair.

"Now, Louise, set the little man at the top, and when I say 'GO' let him go. Okay?"

I eased the board back down.

"GO!"

Louise opened her hand, releasing the little man who somersaulted all the way to the bottom! Kathy watched, having laid the seed pod on the bed.

"Now it's my turn!" she said eagerly.

I raised the board back up, and Kathy put the man down at the top.

"GO!" I whispered loudly, as I lowered the board.

They took two more turns each, marveling at each performance as daylight faded. Kathy slid the little man back in his sack, pulling the strings tight, and returned him to the trunk, along with the flute and seed pod.

"Maybe next time we'll have time to look at some of the children's books that had belonged to Rev and Manny," I muttered to anyone who might be listening. The illustrations always stirred my imagination. It didn't bother me that they were disquieting and bizarre. My favorite was Feodor Rojankofsky's *Animal Stories*. Who would ever have imagined an elephant sitting on eggs, to hatch, no less!

As I lowered the trunk lid we heard Rev slowly making her way up the creaky stairs. "Well, well. I see you're all ready for bed!"

I said, "Revy, we haven't brushed our teeth or washed up yet because we were looking in the trunk and found the little man with the silk suit. We just had to play with him!"

The ritual of getting ready for bed at Rev and Manny's was delightful. It was like being in a foreign land. Having no electricity made us more aware that light was fading and, unless there was a moon, it would soon be dark—except for the trillions of stars in the heavens above.

Kathy and Louise darted into their room followed by Rev and me. Rev poured water from a blue enameled pitcher into the white wash bowls, handing us each a washcloth and small, oval lavender-scented soap to wash our hands and face. Then came my favorite part of the getting-ready-for-bed ritual: brushing our teeth with a dash of Dr. Lyons Tooth Powder. We poured it into the curled palm of one hand, then, with a moistened toothbrush, scraped the bristles across our palm, gathering as much powder as possible. I helped Louise as her hands were too small to maneuver the can of Dr. Lyons. Rev then poured water into each of the jelly jars so we could swish our mouths with water, which we then spit out into the "emergency" pot.

"Don't forget to rinse out your brush and glass with water," Rev reminded us, as she poured more water from the pitcher. Rev handed us each a monogrammed towel from the wash stand, watching our every move. Kathy and Louise eagerly climbed into their respective beds as Rev wished them good night.

"Bonne nuit mes enfants!" With a more serious expression and somewhat provocatively she added, "Try not to disturb the blue goose when you come downstairs tomorrow morning." She gave me a questioning look, as though trying to read whether I sided with her or not.

Rev walked out of the room with a cheerful, "Goodnight, dears!"

With the admonition not to disturb the blue goose, Kathy and Louise pulled their bedspreads over their heads.

"I don't think there's a blue goose and, if there is, he can't get out of the north room," I said. "You can come out from under the covers now! Let's say our prayers before I go back to my room."

I sat on the edge of Louise's bed and we recited in unison: Now I lay me down to sleep... then God bless... independently we named all the people and pets we could think of. Louise was asleep before she'd named everyone on her list.

I tiptoed to my room and crawled into the three-quarter bed, pulling the sheet and blanket to my chin. Something scurried across the roof overhead. Barred owls hooted in the tall pines on the hill across the road. I threw off the covers, slid out of bed and crept over to the east-facing window where I held back Revy's hand-sewn curtain to better see the sky, ablaze with stars. Awed with sights and sounds, I soon slipped back into bed and fell asleep.

Early the next morning, I awoke to my sisters playing quietly in their room with their stuffed companions. "Let's get dressed and be ready to go," I whispered. I went back to my room and did the same.

We packed up our bags to go home for breakfast. Rev and Manny had an icebox for refrigeration and I'd stayed at their house enough to remain suspicious—especially of milk. Rev, never one to waste anything, would pour soured milk into a linen cloth bag and hang it over a bowl, letting the whey drain from the curds. The result was cottage cheese that bore only a faint resemblance to the cottage cheese we had at home.

Rev lit a fire in the cookstove and was getting ready to make the morning coffee from dark-roasted coffee beans she'd freshly ground in the grinder that hung beside the cellar door. Manny cleared his throat as he waited in bed for Rev to bring him a cup of French coffee.

Knowing how we loved using that grinder, Rev brought a chair for us to stand on while we took turns turning the wooden handle that moved the steel shaft, creating a circular motion that moved the gears that ground the beans. Once ground Rev emptied the tin container on the grinder into a glass jar to make tomorrow's coffee. "Thank you, Revy!" we uttered, more or less in unison. We picked up our overnight bags and continued through the living room, into the vestibule and out the front door without having awakened Gambo, who was still sleeping.

Our bare feet touched the granite steps, warmed by the early morning sun. A perfect beginning to a new day! The swallows had already migrated south; and in the distance we heard the distinctive call of the pileated woodpecker.

————————

As we made our way toward the path home, we hastened our pace as we passed the north room window, home of the questionable blue goose. I glanced at the window as we raced by and saw no sign of a big blue bird. I still wasn't entirely convinced that it didn't exist. I needed proof.

Louise, with her pony in one arm, grabbed Kathy's hand as we raced along the path toward home. That blue goose added a thrill for me, albeit a scary one. But it instilled terror in Louise and Kathy.

At home we were met with the aroma of fresh toast and coffee. Mummy greeted us as she set the table for our first meal of the day.

"Did you have a nice time?"

Kathy answered first. "Yeah, but the blue goose is really scary!"

I wasn't sure what I wanted to hear for an answer, so I asked if there *really* was a blue goose.

Mummy didn't seem to understand how frightened we all were. "The blue goose is Manny's way of trying to get Louise to stop sucking her thumb."

I hoped for a more dramatic answer. Maybe that there was a blue goose! But our mother seldom engaged in drama; rather she maintained her cool, rational attitude, appearing to have few irrational fears—except spiders, and she tried, with only fleeting moments of success, to see spiders the way her friend Laura Barr Lougee wrote and illustrated them in *The Web of the Spider*.

I returned to the Raffy's that afternoon. Mummy's explanation, although plausible, didn't convince Kathy and Louise. It was Mummy's word against Manny's, and a blue goose that would snap off a thumb was an odious thought. It was several months before they went back to the Raffy's—when most geese had flown south.

Stop the Horses

Raffy's field, where we often pastured our horses, was about a thousand feet away from our home. Revy, in charge since Mummy was away, decided that it was time for the horses to go home. She asked my sisters and me to stand on the gravel road with our arms extended, to "STOP THE HORSES!" To complete the picture:

I was 9!

Kathy was 6!

Louise was just 4!

As Rev slid back the bars the horses seized the chance to head for home, knowing grain was waiting in their buckets. As we stood on the road, all three of them came galloping toward us; we did what anyone would have done: we jumped out of the way! Rev came huffing toward us from the gate—not to see if we were okay, but to chastise us for not stopping the horses!

We followed the horses back to the barn where they had already gone into their stalls and were nuzzling their buckets as they ate their grain. Kathy and Louise went into the stalls to pat the horses before I secured the latches.

Rev's darker side revealed itself when situations were not to her liking. This time, she lowered her voice in a haughty, Boston accent to make her pronouncement:

There shall be NO-O-O Christmas this year!

Two or three weeks later Rev was standing, barefoot, in our kitchen. I noticed that she had a curved black and blue horseshoe-shaped imprint on the side of her face. While I wondered if she had made a connection with what she had demanded of us, I did not mention it and neither did she.

Had I questioned the bruise on her face she would have said, "Zippoo, it's nothing—nothing whatsoever!"

Bobby

Bobby Mouton was the only friend I had who was my age, until I went to school. His family spent summer and fall weekends at their camp on Bickford Pond, about a half mile from our house. I loved being with Bobby, in what seemed to be an ideal setting, with an abundance of time, food and drink (sodas for children and alcohol and sodas for adults). The Moutons worked hard and enjoyed investing money on things they coveted: a console radio and phonograph; a motor boat that would pull up to three water skiers; and a dock wide enough for adults to lounge on while overseeing the comings and goings of the younger generation.

Bobby and I became fast friends while looking for worms in the rich, black soil in his backyard; I liked how it felt against my bare feet. Our worm digging was likely encouraged by Bobby's dad, an avid fisherman, who was always looking for bait. While I enjoyed finding wiggly pink bodies, after a few worm-digging sessions I became distracted by other things, like tadpoles and wild flowers. I recalled that Bobby's mother, Ada, had mentioned that foxgloves grew "out back" at the camp, and while I had no idea what to look for, I liked the word *foxgloves* and the image it conjured.

Once, feeling adventurous, I left Bobby digging beside

the driveway and walked to the back of the camp where, just a few feet from the lake were tall plants covered with pinkish, bell-shaped blossoms with purple dots inside the bells. *These must be foxgloves since the only others are Sweet William!* The blossoms hung there, asking to be picked, so I yielded to temptation and placed a bell on each finger to make my own gloves. The whole idea was thrilling as I picked one blossom at a time, one for each finger. I couldn't wait to show Bobby. With my hands stretched out before me I shouted excitedly, "See my new gloves!" He stopped digging to come take a closer look. Then he wanted some too!

"Come with me. I'll show you how you can make some!"

At the time I obviously had no idea that Digitalis was a powerful heart stimulant derived from foxgloves. And Bobby's mother, Ada, must have been unaware of their danger as well, since she never mentioned that they weren't to be eaten or that we shouldn't put our hands in our mouths after handling them.

———

Before going to the Moutons I knew that my chores had to be done—no short-cuts. I liked the responsibility of chores, and liked knowing my parents knew where I would be and what Bobby and I planned to be doing. The latter was easy because whatever we did invariably involved fishing.

On one of our fishing expeditions along the Pearl Brook I carried the can of worms and Bobby's string of brook trout while Bobby fished. Meanwhile, black flies and mosquitoes feasted on my exposed skin. When the black flies were especially ferocious, I consoled myself by acknowledging that at least I wasn't fishing on moss-covered rocks in a flowing brook.

When Bobby asked if the black flies were biting I yelled back, "Now what do you think? One more bite and I'm leaving!" Bobby found this amusing. "Just one more brook trout and I'll be ready to leave, too!"

"This is NOT FUN!" I yelled back. All at once there was a kerfuffle and a splash. "Are you okay?" I shouted.

"Next time I won't wear these boots!" said Bobby, as he hauled himself out of the brook.

"*Now* are you ready to leave?" I asked impatiently. I could see that he wasn't hurt, though he continued to sputter. "What about your boots? You aren't going to walk back barefoot, are you?"

I turned to walk toward the road while he yanked on his wet boots. He followed behind, clearly annoyed with himself. As we approached the embankment at the edge of the road, I hoped to get a rise out of Bobby. "Yesterday, when I was on my bike, a bear cub ran across the road right in front of me. Right here!" I said, easing my way down the embankment.

"What's that?" Bobby asked.

"Yesterday I saw a bear cub right here on my way to your camp. I was riding my bike."

Bobby laughed. "Then Mama's long gone... baby cub too."

I stopped. "But I didn't see a Mama bear. I only saw a cub. It ran right in front of my bike."

Bobby, still dripping, had caught up and was walking beside me. "Well," he joshed, "You may not have seen her, but she saw you!"

"How do you know?" I asked.

"Because I know about bears!"

———

Bobby had access to his Dad's old twelve-foot, wide-beamed, wooden boat with a five-horsepower motor; occasionally, with enough pulling, choking and adjusting, it even started. While Bobby cranked the motor I paddled with an oar, watching for a good fishing hole. Once found, one of us dropped the anchor overboard with a mighty splash that roiled the sediment. After it settled, we watched for underwater life: sunfish, perch, pickerel and painted turtles. One of our most thrilling underwater sightings was a loon passing directly beneath the boat, like a torpedo. "Did you see that!" I shrieked. Holding the fishing line between his teeth as he added a hook, Bobby let the line fall onto his leg, while still holding the hook. "I've never seen a loon swim under a boat in all my time on the pond," he said. "It might be a sign we're near some fish!"

Time seemed endless as we cast for any fish that might bite. When either of us brought a fish into the boat, Bobby removed the hook and released the fish back into the water. I really didn't like any part of removing hooks, watching the fish wriggle and squirm. I soon wondered about the whole idea of fishing—unless they were going to be eaten. *Why bother catching fish if you're just going to throw them back?*

———

Bobby didn't have scheduled chores, although he was occasionally asked to help his mother or Gram Blazo make lunch. His freedom was based on mutual trust between him and his parents. With that respect came the expectation that he would earn his pocket money. By the summer of his thirteenth year his great uncle Sam, overseer of the Porter Village Cemetery, gave Bobby a job digging graves and maintaining the grounds. In some ways it was a perfect job: he had to work only six to eight hours a week; he could choose which days to work; and he didn't have to work under the supervision of anyone but Sam, who made clear his expectations and trusted Bobby to carry them out, one grave at a time.

"Say Zip, why don't you come down to the cemetery to visit sometime?" Bobby asked. "Then you can see what I do." That sounded like a plan. The following week, with Mum's permission, I set out for Porter Village on my bike, picking my way around potholes and stones on Colcord Pond Road, then on County Road. It was a four-mile ride, up and down steep hills much of the way. Luckily it was mid-week and only two or three cars passed by, both coming from the opposite direction.

The cemetery was situated on the hillside behind Herb and Lil MacDonald's Corner Store. The cemetery entrance was halfway down the hill. To make the right turn into the cemetery, I had to stand on my bike pedals to slow down enough to turn into the cemetery. From the gate I could see Bobby at the right upper end, bent over shoveling, gravel and rocks flying from the gravesite. He didn't see me until I called out. "Hi! I'm here!" I lay my bike down next to the entrance and walked to where Bobby was working.

"So, you actually dug all this out today? You really do work hard, don't you?"

Bobby leaned on his shovel, then stood up to dig some more. "You can sit over there, beside that headstone. I gotta keep digging or Sam will fire me. You don't mind, do you?" He chuckled.

"Of course not. I came to see what you actually do and now I have a good idea. And, I don't mind watching." I felt that I was digging right along with him as beads of sweat collected on his upper lip. "Aren't you hot?"

"Now whadda you think? This is back-breaking work, but I only have to break my back three or four hours, twice a week; the rest of the time is my own. Think I'll start a little earlier next time, though!"

The air smelled of hot skin and dried earth. Thunderheads were building up in the west. Bobby's shirt was drenched when I put my hand on his shoulder. "Guess I'd better head home before the storm gets here. Bobby, is your Dad going to pick you up?"

Bobby leaned on his spade as a grin spread across his face. "He'll be here soon—if Mother doesn't nab him first! You know how she always has a list of things for Dad to do!"

Hank Rutherford

Pink water lilies bobbed in the cove near Hank's new shingled, eight-by-eight miniature house with gabled ends, perched on a point on the southern end of Bickford Pond, where from his wee kitchen window he had a prime view of the lilies. Fidgety and eccentric, in his late 60s, Hank was about 5'6" with a slight build. He shaved regularly but always missed a few stray whiskers. His droopy mustache and shoulder-length, gray hair seemed consistent with his halting, quavery speech. His clothes, largely threadbare, had once been of high quality.

Twice a month Hank drove his white, 1939 Ford coupe to town for provisions. After a few "episodes" it didn't take long for shop owners to brace themselves for his arrival. He was known to have violent outbursts when an item he wanted was out of stock, once swiping paint cans off the shelf at Ridlon's Market when his choice of paint was unavailable.

Being a recluse, visitors were not welcome in "Hank's Kingdom." This made his invitation to Bobby and me all the more intriguing. So it was with a sense of urgency (lest he change his mind) that we hastily planned our trip. We were eleven, curious and intrigued by this curmudgeon. We'd had numerous "off-shore visits" with him, but this was an opportunity for us to come for tea.

Bobby made arrangements with Hank for us to come mid-morning, on a weekday when the pond was relatively quiet. Bobby clocked the time it took to get to Hank's from his camp, on a calm day, at eight minutes.

———

On the chosen day Bobby eased his boat into Hank's cove and cut the motor, tilting it up to avoid getting the motor stuck in layers of silt. I struggled to get a good foothold. "Grab the oar and push us in," he commanded. *Easier said than done.* With a firm grip on the oar I pushed us to shore with a command of my own, "Hold on! I'm going to give it an extra shove!"

Bobby, barefoot, jumped out of the boat. His pant legs got wet, but who cared? He didn't! He took the end of the thick, braided rope attached to the bow and tied it to a poplar sapling with a half-hitch knot. "Don't think anyone's going to steal it, do you?" he joked.

We walked to the front (and only) door. Bobby urged, "You knock."

"No. You! You know him better than I do," I said, easing back. "*You* knock."

"I'll try this," Bobby said, taking a brass bell from its resting place above the door.

He jiggled the bell gently. "Anybody home?"

Slowly the door opened. "Well, er um [cough] yes. Er... come in..."

Hank looked from Bobby's face to his feet, which had remnants of sand, silt and dead leaves sticking to them. "But first rinse off those feet!" Bobby excused himself and ran back to the lake to dunk his feet in the water. He was careful to stay on the grass on the way back.

Once we were inside, Hank's eyes were still focused on Bobby's muddy feet. I had all I could do to keep from exploding with laughter. We remained standing, cheek by jowl, when Hank sputtered, "Well, well, er, uh, would you care for a cup of tea?" Bobby and I exchanged glances. "Sure, if it won't be too much trouble," I said, looking around to see where I'd place my tea cup since there wasn't even room to sit down!

Bobby grinned, "Guess I might as well have some too."

Before turning around to prepare the tea Hank looked at me and patted the thin upper mattress of the bunk bed behind us. "You sit up here," he said, sliding a small ladder from the wall and attaching it to two hooks on the top bunk. "Bobby and I, er-uh, will sit here, on my bed," he said, patting the lower mattress.

I climbed the ladder, ducking to avoid hitting my head. With Bobby and me situated, Hank walked clumsily to the kitchen, just a few steps away. There was a small propane stove atop a cabinet with shelving. Hank reached into the cabinet for his strike-anywhere, wooden matches, took one from the box and swiped the match against the edge of the box, before it burst into flame. Muttering, he turned the stove's knob to release propane. With a whoosh the propane burned beneath the tea kettle.

Hank returned and put the ladder back on the wall. We'd been so mesmerized watching how Hank lived in this tiny space, that we'd grown silent. And it took a lot to silence Bobby! " I guess I should have done that for you," Bobby said.

In response to Bobby's offer to help, Hank replied haltingly, "Yes, well I do have something you may be able to help me with... er, uh, after our tea."

Hank went back to the kitchen and fetched three, bite-sized, pinwheel-shaped cookies from a blue and yellow tin. He carefully placed them on a floral plate, turned, took about two steps and held the plate up for me. "Take one," he said, before setting the plate on the bed beside Bobby.

The kettle began to whistle, and Hank hustled to shut off the propane before placing a spoonful of loose leaf tea in a metal tea ball which he then lowered to steep in the bottom of a porcelain teapot. He set three china cups on the shelf beside the stove while Bobby and I nibbled at our cookies. Drinking tea from the top bunk meant holding the cup while hunched over since there was no place to set the cup down. Hank and Bobby sat on the lower bunk, sipping their tea while I tried not to spill mine. Bobby held his cup with his joint-less little finger protruding, "Say, Hank. Have you taken your sailing kayak out lately?"

"Well, er, no, it's become more than I can handle. And the mice have been gnawing away at the sails —you might say the kayak now belongs to the mice. Yes, ur um... Yes."

When we finished our tea Hank brought our empty cups to the mini-sink where he left them in an aluminum dishpan. My arms were finally free to help me balance enough to look around. Against one wall was a plaster casting of a naked woman, about a foot high. *Does he know her? Is she dead? Why is she up here?* The intrigue was killing me!

Hank fussed in the kitchen while I whispered, "Bobby, you should see what I've just discovered! A sculpture of a naked woman!" Luckily Bobby hadn't attempted to see for himself because suddenly Hank was back, taking the ladder from the wall so I could climb down. *Did he know*

I'd seen the naked woman?! As he led us out the door I asked if we could see his refrigerator in the brook. It had intrigued me when he mentioned it in an earlier conversation. "That reminds me, ur, um, Bobby I was going to ask you to help me move the cage to a different spot where there's more shade."

We walked about fifteen yards to the small stream where he'd built a wooden arch bridge that gave him access to his Rube Goldberg refrigeration contraption: a cage made of heavy-gauge fencing wire hanging from the bridge and submerged in the icy water. "Bobby, when I raise the cage I want you to grab hold of it. Then we'll move it so it's in the shade." He coughed. "Lately the sun's been beating down on the cage for most of the day. My food will spoil."

Bobby agreed. "That's a problem," he said, holding onto the cage as he looked around. "How about on this side— where it will be shaded by those alder bushes at least part of the day?" Hank stopped to consider Bobby's suggestion, agreeing to give it a try.

"Before you lower that cage, I want to check on the butter and cheese," Hank said, lifting the door to where the tins and jars with foodstuffs were stored. He coughed again. "Make sure they haven't turned rancid."

He opened the container with butter and sniffed, "It's okay!" The next container held cheddar cheese. "This is okay as well. Hand me that milk." When he unscrewed the jar he didn't have to sniff. "As I thought," he said. "So sour it's curdled."

Because Hank trusted few people, knowing that his refrigeration system was hidden from view and intentionally complicated gave him a certain comfort. After we sufficiently admired his ingenuity, he said, "You youngsters had better be getting along."

"I'll be back someday soon, to see if the new location is working out any better for you," Bobby said. "Thanks a lot."

"Thanks for tea and for showing us how you keep your food cold," I added. Hank watched us as we shoved the boat into the water and climbed aboard. We waved and Hank waved back before he went inside.

Once out of earshot, Bobby said, "I don't think too many people would believe us if we told them about Hank! To think that he has no electricity and no phone, and he doesn't seem to mind!"

"I agree. No one would believe us if we described him," I said. "You do know that he doesn't stay here all winter, don't you?"

"Well, I figured he'd freeze to death if he did, so yeah, I guess I knew he didn't spend winters here!"

"Rev said he stays at the Hotel Malvern in Kezar Falls, the New Lincoln in Cornish and, every now and then, at The Eastland Hotel in Portland. He and Rev write to each other sometimes, and once a summer he stops in for a visit."

I reached for an oar to shove us off while Bobby primed the engine. "Do you think Hank would mind if we got a couple of those pink water lilies to plant down in your cove?" I asked.

"We're not getting them today, even if he would approve! But, I don't think he'd mind. Although, he seems to think he was the first person to grow them on Bickford Pond."

"Wasn't Lucy Waite the person who introduced pink water lilies to Bickford Pond? And didn't she give Hank his first pink water lily tubers?"

Bobby pulled the cord, and the engine started. We headed off, down the pond, with yet another story to tell.

Death's Mystery

When Beauty, our old black mare, had to be put down, Dad, with the help of two neighbors, dug a horse-size grave in a nearby esker. With a man on either side, Dad walked Beauty a half mile along the dirt road to the hole they'd dug. An hour later Dad returned with his head lowered and his eyes squinted. I quietly asked, "How did Beauty die, Dad?"

"She was still standing when she died," Dad said solemnly.

"But *how* did she die?"

"I injected her vein with saline solution, a mixture of salt and water," Dad answered. "She didn't feel a thing."

"How do you know that?" I asked. "If she needed to be put down, how could she have walked that far? Do you think she knew she was about to die?"

With a furrowed brow, my father's eyes met mine. "Beauty was old and sick. We did what was best." He walked to the sink and reached into the cupboard below for Bon Ami, the all-purpose cleaner. Dad turned on the faucet and a thin stream of water flowed as he shook Bon Ami from the gold can into his right palm. He slowly worked the soap along the top of his hands, along his arms, front and back. I stood behind him as he washed and washed, wondering what he could possibly be scrubbing off. His arms didn't appear to be *that* dirty.

To Kelly's Market

At the edge of the field behind our house was the garden—where my sisters and I each had small plots. We planted, tended and raised radishes, tomatoes, carrots, green beans and summer squash to sell at Kelly's Market. In mid-late summer, when our veggies had ripened, we harvested our "bounty" in baskets made of wooden splints, much too large for four-year-old Louise to carry. Kathy and I carried ours in front of our bodies, and Daddy carried Louise's. "Before we leave, make a quick run to the bathroom. Then we'll drive downtown to Kelly's."

Mr. Kelly greeted us warmly in his spiffy attire: a white dress shirt, a straw hat with a black ribbon above the brim, wing-tipped shoes, trousers and a clean white apron. He admired and weighed our produce, selecting what he could sell, which was everything we had in our baskets! With a pencil and paper, he figured out what he owed us and gave each of us a third of the earnings in coins. Dad encouraged us to save our money, but on this hot day, as a special treat, he suggested we get ice cream at Ridlon's Pharmacy.

Eager for our treats, Kathy, Louise and I walked along the sidewalk from Kelly's Market, across the bridge spanning the Ossipee River, to the pharmacy. Dad had errands at the post office and at Carl Hammond's Jewelry Shop, up a long flight of stairs and above the post office.

Once at Ridlon's, I tugged on the door latch and a two-toned bell announced our arrival. Iva, Mr. Ridlon's assistant, called out from the back room, "Be right with ya!" She and Mr. Ridlon were putting up prescriptions in the back room. I helped Louise onto her stool and then we sat twirling on stools covered in gray marbled vinyl, as the ceiling fan whirred above us. Louise couldn't reach the floor to twirl her stool, but she caught sight of the stuffed fox and weasel on a high shelf above the magazine rack. "I see a fox!" she said with surprise. When Iva finally emerged from the back room, standing behind the counter, she asked, "What can I do for you girls?" Being so focused on twirling, we hadn't thought about what flavors we wanted. In the end we each chose a different flavor: vanilla, strawberry and chocolate ice cream cones, all small. All with jimmies.

Iva bent over the deep freezer chest to scoop out Louise's strawberry ice cream to fill her sugar cone; she sprinkled jimmies on top. Louise held out her left hand and Iva handed her the cone. "Don't eat it all at once," Iva kidded. Next, she prepared Kathy's chocolate ice cream cone, asking if she also wanted jimmies. "Yes, please!" Kathy said, reaching for her cone. She immediately licked off all her jimmies. Finally, Iva scooped vanilla ice cream into the last cone, sprinkled it with jimmies and handed it to me. "Sooo good!" I said, licking my ice cream while pushing it into the cone with my tongue.

"That'll be five cents each," Iva said, waiting as we dug, with our sticky hands, into our pockets for our nickels. We must have been covered with ice cream because Iva said, "Now you girls need a bath!" as she put our nickels into the cash register.

Iva was friendly but seemed impatient as we lingered on the stools. She trotted back and forth with a dishcloth, swiping at stray spills on the counter. "I suppose you girls will be going back to school pretty soon." Kathy and I rolled our eyes at the thought. I mumbled, "Yeah. Louise doesn't go to school yet, though. She's only four." For some reason, I found this amusing; when I caught Kathy's attention we fought to contain our giggles that were about to erupt. With our heads slightly lowered, we glanced at each other and I nodded—a signal that we should leave right away. I helped Louise down from the stool, and we bolted toward the door leaving our stool seats spinning.

"Now we get to go back across the bridge to find Daddy! He's probably talking with Malcolm, Eula, Win, Jiddy or Gordon at the bank or with Jimmy and Paul at Howe's Plumbing and Heating." I was pretty sure we'd find him.

"There's Daddy in the Jeep, right out front! We don't have to wait for him after all!" Kathy shouted, running to the Jeep.

Once we were all in the back seat Daddy suggested, "What do you say we go home and go for a swim!" Iva was right. We did need a bath!

Charlotte Giovanella Fullam

Only our Maker could create
The panorama of a sunset
With its glowing rays of light
Slowly then, the bright shades deepen
To blue-lavender, then
Twilight

Charlotte, age 12

Adolescence

Charlotte Giovanella Fullam

Rustling on Kennard Hill

Merle shifted the bus into low gear as he approached the corner where the gravel road made a steep descent to the valley below. Beside the road a gurgling brook flowed down from the mountainside, under the bridge between great slabs of granite. Just beyond the bridge was the Weeks' farm where Lorraine lived with her parents.

After a long school day I looked forward to the ride home looking out the bus windows. On this day I sat on the driver's side, and my sisters were playing with a Slinky toward the back of the bus, oblivious that we were nearly home.

We were on our way down the steep hill on the Maine-New Hampshire border when an old gray sedan approached. The car caught my eye because the driver was wearing sunglasses, something more unusual to see in spring than late fall when the sun was low on the horizon. And I noticed someone in the passenger seat but couldn't see whether it was a woman or a man. Merle stopped the bus as far off the road as he dared, avoiding the gully, to make room for the car to pass. Sensing the tight quarters, Merle raised his right arm, motioning the driver to come ahead, then quickly bent his hand straight up and back down, repeatedly, indicating s-l-o-w d-o-w-n.

As the car passed beneath my window I peered into the

back seat and noticed that it was covered with a sheet. What appeared to be a broom handle protruded through the sheet. *That's odd.* I looked again and on closer inspection saw that it wasn't a broom handle, but rather the barrel of a rifle! The car continued up the hill and I wondered if it would turn left toward Porter Village or right into New Hampshire. It turned right, up Rice Hill and disappeared from sight.

Saying nothing to anyone about the rifle, I summoned Nancy Drew and committed the license plate number to memory, repeating the number until the bus stopped in front of our house. My sisters and I stepped down with the usual, "See you tomorrow!" I'd just witnessed something that both scared and excited me. I had a mystery to solve!

My sisters ate their snacks while I went upstairs to change my clothes. Being black-fly season, I put on a long-sleeved polo shirt and dungereens, a word coined by Gram Hadlock that had quickly caught on with my sisters and me.

I hurried downstairs, grabbed a cookie and raced to the front door, nearly running into Gram coming in from the clothesline with a basket of clothes. "Sorry, Gram! Where's Dad?" I asked, coughing on inhaled cookie crumbs.

"He's feeding the cattle up on Kennard Hill," she said. "He should be home any time now."

Not wanting to waste even a second, I shouted, "Gram, tell Kathy and Louise that I'm going out to do my chores." The door slammed behind me.

"Haven't I told you not to let the door slam?"

"Sorry, Gram!" I said as I dashed to the barn.

I liked scooping urine sawdust and manure into the wheelbarrow, emptying the barrow on the manure pile, and refilling it with fresh sawdust for each stall. I forgot all about the rifle and creepy car... until Dad came home. I dropped the shovel and ran to meet him. Instead of a warm greeting he said, "Wait right here, honey. I must call Vern." *Why did he need to call the game warden?*

When he was back, Dad's eyebrows were still furrowed. "Something's very wrong." Dad said and cleared his throat. "When I brought grain to the Drowns' pasture this afternoon, two cattle were missing. I wouldn't have thought much about it except that they always come when I bring their grain. Then, as I walked through the field and into the woods looking for them, I spotted blood on some dead leaves along the path. Then more blood on a patch of moss near the brook. But there was no sign of the cattle so I figured someone must have shot them and..."

"Shot! With a gun?!" I asked, connecting the pieces of the puzzle. "Dad, I think I can help! Coming home on the school bus an old gray car was on its way past the bus on the steep hill near the New Hampshire line. I saw a gun sticking up through a sheet covering the back seat! Because it looked so suspicious I memorized the license plate. It was a white Maine plate with 282-841 in black; mud was splattered all over it." I was talking so fast Dad asked, "Zip. Would you repeat that? Not quite so fast this time."

I began again. "I have the license plate number!" While I explained again what I'd seen, Vern's black sedan pulled into the dooryard. He opened the door and slowly got out. Dad walked over to greet him.

"Vern, so good of you to make the trip up here."

Vern dropped his cigarette and wiggled the toe of his shoe back and forth on top of the butt, snuffing the embers. It wasn't uncommon for Vern to stop in for a visit after a day of fishing on Colcord Pond, but today was different. He was here on business. In his baritone voice he explained, "We have a problem in that whoever was involved likely drove from here into New Hampshire. It may take time to coordinate with out of state law enforcement."

Dad put his hand on my shoulder. "This young lady has some valuable information. Zip, tell Vern what you told me. Slowly tell him what you saw, one step at a time." I began, "I first noticed that an old gray car was going sort of fast when it met the school bus. The car was really dirty... and the driver looked weird. He wore sunglasses, the kind we call "shades." There was a sheet covering the back seat, and a rifle was sticking up through the sheet. The license plate on the car was white with Maine, 1951, 282-841 in black." Vern jotted the information in his notebook as I spoke.

"That information will certainly be helpful as we try to locate the car and the poachers," Vern said. "Would you give me the license number again, slowly." I repeated, "282-841."

"Whatever made you think you should remember that license plate?"

"That's easy; I've read most of the Nancy Drew mysteries at the Kezar Falls Library!"

"Well, that's quite a story. Maybe more youngsters should read Nancy Drew mysteries," Vern said, turning to Dad, rubbing his chin. "Joe, you mind if I use your phone to call in this information. It should speed up the recovery of the car, and there's even a slim chance we could retrieve the meat."

Vern was one of many people who called my dad by the first part of our last name, mistakenly thinking Giovanella was Joe Vanilla. It was easy to understand why since Dad often answered the phone: "Giovanella, here."

Dad gestured to Vern, "You know where the phone is, Vern. Go right in, and don't worry about long-distance charges. The sooner this crime is solved, the better. Thanks to Zip's quick thinking, I believe the poachers will be found—if not in hours, then in days!"

I was bursting with pride, and my face ached from the smile that felt permanently stitched from cheek to cheek. Dad and I followed Vern into the house and walked to the family room where Dad sat down in the easy chair with his newspaper. I went to the bookcase and randomly chose a volume from our new set of World Book Encyclopedias. I stretched out on the sofa and thumbed through the pages, stopping to read captions beneath pictures that caught my eye.

When Vern finished speaking with the State Police in both Maine and New Hampshire, he came to the doorway, glanced at Dad and me, both of us reading. "Thanks, Joe. I'll be on my way. Helen will have dinner ready by the time I get to the village." Dad folded the newspaper and placed his hands on the arms of the chair, as he started to rise.

"Stay right there, Joe. No need to get up. You'll be hearing from me shortly. Thank *you*, young lady!" Vern turned to leave, and Dad settled back in his easy chair, calling out, "I appreciate all your effort, Vern!"

Gram, who had been sewing, stepped from her room wearing a well-worn, cotton apron. "It's time I got some supper on the table. I made a beef stew this morning. All I need to do is heat it up and add a few carrots. Zippy, would you go upstairs and get your sisters to come down to help you set the table?"

After supper, I was watching the news with Dad when the phone rang. Dad usually let me answer, but he said, "I'd better take this call; it's probably Vern." He rose from his chair and picked up the phone in the little room.

"Hello... Yes. Vern, good to hear from you. ... They did? ... Where? ... It was? ... She'll be happy to know that. Let me know if there's anything I can do. ... What? ... No! Guess it's a good thing I didn't go farther into the woods. I might have been carved up, too!... I can't thank you enough for all your help. Speak with you soon."

Dad returned to the family room, "With the information you gave Vern they've already nabbed the poachers."

I wasn't sure what "nabbed" meant.

"You mean they caught the poachers?"

"They sure did." Dad said, grinning.

Wanting still more information, I asked, "What did you mean when you said you could've been carved up, too?"

Dad cleared his throat. "The poachers told the officers they'd been ready to shoot me had I gone any farther into the woods. They were carving up one of the carcasses as I walked toward them—only I didn't know they were there. I figured that whoever had killed the cattle had done so earlier that day."

"Dad? What would have happened if I hadn't noticed the car and hadn't memorized the license plate number?"

"It's hard to say, but I'm pretty sure the poachers might have escaped. At the very least it would have taken a lot longer to find their car. With the information you gave, the police were able to put out an alert with the car description, including the Maine license plate number. It only took a couple of hours for police to find the car parked along a side road in Berwick. While police questioned them, the poachers explained they'd gone to Rochester, New Hampshire and drove back roads to downtown Berwick. That's where they abandoned their car."

"What did they do with the meat?" I asked.

Dad picked up the newspaper. "That's a good question. They may have sold it by the time they got to Berwick."

"It's creepy to think that you were so near the thieves, Dad. That they could have shot you!"

Dad gave the newspaper a shake, then straightened it.

"I'm just glad those thieves will go to jail," I offered.

"Not quite so fast! They may or may not go to jail," Dad explained. "First there will be a trial. When all the evidence has been presented, the judge or a jury will decide the case. But no matter what happens to the rustlers, you were a darn good detective!"

Dad went back to his newspaper while I sat up on the couch, "I can't wait to tell Mummy when she gets home!"

Hot Air Balloon

Ballooning over Black Mountain in a basket propelled by hot air, was an adventure Bobby had been incubating since he'd read about it in one of his magazines. With help from his dad he worked out some of the details, like the cost of a balloon in an Army Surplus catalog. There was, however, a major obstacle: the cost of helium to fill the balloon. When he asked me if I'd ride in the basket with him, it was with the understanding that we'd split the cost. That said, my allowance wasn't going to cover the helium, even if we combined our allowances for five years!

Trying to ease Bobby's disappointment I offered a few worst-case scenarios: What if we had a leak or got hung up on electric lines or landed in a lake or were blown off course into the path of a plane?

To my relief, we never did find an affordable source for helium. Bobby's dream had been thwarted, and I felt sorry for his disappointment but was convinced that we'd been saved from a catastrophe, because when asked to go on adventure, I seldom refused.

Geraldine

Every summer Geraldine moved with her parents, grandmother and younger brother, Larry, to their family's summer cottage on a nearby pond. While her parents worked at full-time jobs their grandmother kept a watchful eye over Geraldine and Larry, insisting that they remain within sight of their cottage. At all times.

Given that trees and underbrush surrounded their cottage on three sides, they were mostly confined to working on picture puzzles on a table in the living room. On rare occasions, on her way to work, Geraldine's mother dropped her off at my house. One summer's day, instead of playing badminton or croquet or riding Tony, Geraldine asked me to photograph her. I'd been given a Brownie Hawkeye box camera for Christmas and liked taking pictures of my friends. We were both eleven, but had different interests. Geraldine was more mature and wanted to talk about boys, while I was still happy to explore out of doors or be in the tree house with Lorraine, waiting for the cows to bunch together below our perch in the pasture pine.

In our tiny upstairs bathroom, there was just enough room for Geraldine to pose in front of the medicine cabinet mirror while I balanced on the toilet seat holding my camera and flash attachment, to photograph her from a side angle, thereby avoiding the glare of the flashbulb. Gerry wore a white blouse with the collar pulled up, creating a pleasant contrast to her short black hair, sculpted with water into comma-like shapes around her face. She preened in the mirror, twitched her mouth in various "poses" and asked me to capture her when she looked her best.

I was surprised and admittedly, somewhat flattered, when Bicknell Photo of Portland enclosed a note with the photos, encouraging me to keep working at photography. In retrospect they probably encouraged everyone to keep taking photos because it was good for business!

Camp Laughing Loon

Going to summer camp wasn't a tradition in our family, but in 1952, the summer I turned eleven, Geraldine convinced me that we could go to the same session for two weeks. She went each summer and loved every minute of it. My parents were surprisingly supportive, although they did question why I wasn't content to stay at home where we had horses, a lake and plenty of chores to be done.

Mom and Dad talked it over and agreed that "it might be a good experience" for me (and, perhaps, a break for them). Mom filled out the application form the next morning and mailed it to Camp Laughing Loon in East Waterboro.

Three weeks later my acceptance arrived in the mail, along with a list of required items. There was something about this list I liked. I can still recall the feeling of gathering items from the list, and best of all, looking for clothing at Hanold's, a company in Standish specializing in uniforms and sensible clothing required by camps and schools. Mum drove me to one of their tent sales to buy navy blue shorts, a sweatshirt, socks, a swimsuit and white button-up shirts.

The Sears catalog, along with Ridlon's Pharmacy and Goodwins, had most of the other items: rubber boots, rain slicker, flashlight with batteries, bedding, toothbrush, toothpaste, suntan lotion, shampoo, hair brush and "sundries." It turned out "sundries" meant razors, hair bleach, dye and "feminine items" none of which I had a use for, but no one needed to know that.

At the end of the list were the following instructions: "All clothing must be labeled with the camper's name sewn inside the garment for identification." Mummy ordered them from Loring, Short & Harmon in Portland, and they arrived just a week later with my name printed in blue ink. I asked Mum if she would sew the labels on as soon as possible. She had a better idea: "I'll show you how to sew them on yourself."

Readers, if you are wondering why my mother didn't sew them for me, at that time, I had wondered the same thing. Mum was a firm believer in self-reliance, and she expected her daughters to learn basic skills she had to learn "the hard way" as an adult.

Sewing on name tags proved to be such a tedious process that I began to question whether going to camp would be worth the hours of tiny stitches. Threading the needle seemed impossible until Mum found her needle threader in a crevice of her sewing basket. This simple tool made threading the needle a task anyone could undertake with assured success. Mum showed me how simple it was to use, placing the "u" of the threader through the eye of the needle, then placing enough thread in the "u" and pulling the wire and thread through the eye of the needle. With the tiny needle threaded, holding it in my right hand between my thumb and index finger, I inserted it through the edge of the cotton label. I then caught a few threads of fiber from inside the shirt collar where it was being sewn. "If you pin the label where you plan to sew it, it will remain in place, making the sewing easier," Mum advised.

She was so right. I managed to get all the labels sewn on while it was raining.

————

Sunday afternoons were when "new shifts" of campers arrived. My parents drove me to Camp Laughing Loon, just forty minutes from home, on a rainy day that made pine needles stick to everything. Mum and Dad helped me unload my belongings, gave me advice about being cooperative and, after kissing me goodbye, they wished me well and drove away.

Fortunately, there were lots of "required activities," and before I knew it we were having a meeting in the Rec Hall. It was at this meeting that we were given our assignments for helping out at camp. Wouldn't you know, my job was cleaning the "hoosegow"—not the jail, but the toilet/bath house, which, believe me, wasn't a place where you'd want to spend any extra time! *Nasty job.* I felt a bad attitude beginning to fester.

At Laughing Loon everyone swam. To get placed in the appropriate swim group we had to individually "perform" a series of swimming maneuvers. At home I could swim across the pond (with a boat beside me). However, my legs couldn't perform the scissor kick—no matter how hard I tried. This meant I was relegated to the beginners' area: a couple of feet of water, roped off with buoys where girls who didn't swim could learn. *But I could swim a mile at home! Not fair!* Attitude worsening.

At the end of my first week a canoe/overnight camping trip to an island at the far end of Little Ossipee Lake was announced. One of the Junior Counselors told me that halfway to the island all campers would be asked to show the card that was awarded upon successful completion of the Intermediate Swimmer test.

I felt justified in making this overnight trip because I knew the beginners' area wasn't where I actually belonged. I sensed that I was being treated unfairly and going on this trip was my way of retaliating. I could swim a mile and was an intermediate swimmer, in my estimation. And surely they weren't going to go all the way back if one person didn't have a card! (I was right about that.)

———

Several evenings later, when the campers were in their respective tents, when the only lights were awkward motions of flashlights behind the canvas walls, like colossal fireflies, darting and landing, I listened closely to a conversation in the adjacent tent. An older camper was being picked on. Her name was Cecile. She was born in Québec, and was one of only a handful of girls who were Roman Catholic. Camp Laughing Loon, while a YWCA camp, was largely WASP.

My dad experienced discrimination as a child of Italian immigrants, and was adamant that his children be tolerant of differences. He frequently championed the underdog. In the darkness of that night I felt empowered to sneak to the tent and speak up on her behalf. "Cecile is just as good as anyone else in here," I blurted, following Dad's example.

———

Judy, the Swimming Director, was a strong, graceful swimmer and diver, responsible for all aquatic activities. I was mesmerized watching her perform at a swimming exhibition and was determined to practice kicking with my "legs straight." I was especially intrigued with the spring-board atop the high dive tower. Judy walked out on that springboard with such power and grace, beads of water flowing down her tan body and glistening with oil. As she prepared to dive, she built up a rhythmic pattern at the end of the board. Ta-ta-ta-ta-ta! Ta-ta-ta-ta-ta!

With her arms outstretched, thumbs locked, head lowered she catapulted into space, her body a sleek form, slightly curved as she sliced into the water below, reappearing seconds later with a toss of her head to clear away water. *I'm going to do this—come hell or high water!*

I repeated the sound pattern made by the springboard over and over in my head. I mentioned my intention to no one while I waited for the perfect opportunity to carry out my attempt at diving from the high tower. At the crack of dawn, nearing the end of the second week of camp, I awoke just as daylight was breaking; the world around me was silent. Heavy mist curled around the tent and pines obscuring everything more than twenty feet away. *This is my moment!*

While my tent mates slept I slipped into my bathing suit, grabbed a towel, put my sweatshirt and jeans on over the bathing suit and walked to the waterfront. I tossed the outer layer of clothing onto the damp ground and, without looking back, swam out to the float, deliberately climbed to the top of the tower and walked out onto the diving board. I felt confident that I could dive from the springboard, just like Judy. Standing at the end of the diving board I made the board bounce until I heard the pattern I'd memorized. *Whoa! This is really high!* I was feeling on top of the world as I left the springboard.

I must have twisted the right way because I plunged, head first, into the water like an anchor, down, down, down until my fingers touched the muddy bottom. I shoved off, let my feet drop down and grasped at the water with both hands, climbing back to the water's surface. I began to panic, wondering if I had enough air to keep climbing. I was so relieved when I emerged through the water I nearly forgot to take a deep breath. *Wow! Close call! But sooo worth it!*

I scrambled to get my outer clothes over the wet bathing suit, walked as fast as I could back to the tent and slipped back into bed before anyone woke up.

Babysitting

In the 1950s my parents were active members of the local Parent Teacher Association (PTA). They volunteered with other parents to paint classrooms and hallways, transforming the cavernous, high-ceilinged spaces from dreary pastel orangey-beige walls into lighter, brighter and more inviting environments.

The guest speaker at one of those PTA meetings was the newly appointed principal at Porter High School, A. Raymond "Ray" Rogers. Being witty, charming and well informed, he was passionate about education and life. Simply put, Ray Rogers was good company, or at least my family thought so.

Soon after that PTA meeting Mummy invited Ray, his wife, Jay (whom she hadn't yet met) and their toddler, Brian, to come for a casual Sunday afternoon visit. We walked in the woods, listened to bluejays screeching in the oak trees and noted pileated drillings in dead tree trunks while Brian rode on his father's shoulders. There was an almost instantaneous camaraderie as the families became acquainted. My parents shared stories of their challenges beginning their married life together in Porter, as well as their ongoing challenge of living in the country with each other, neither of whom had roots in Maine or experience in country living.

Both Ray and Jay were recent graduates of Colby College, and it was soon discovered that they shared Mummy's love of books and also read *Saturday Review*, cover to cover. While Daddy wasn't a reader of fiction, he did, nevertheless, keep abreast of news and things that interested him. He enjoyed the Rogers' visits, though perhaps not to quite the extent Mum did.

She clearly enjoyed having friends with whom she shared multiple interests. Her laughter, which had lain nearly dormant for far too long, was heartwarming, especially for her family, for whom her depression was always lurking, if not active.

When I was in seventh grade Mummy asked if I'd consider babysitting with the Rogers' children, Brian and his infant sister, Robin, while they attended a PTA meeting at Milliken School, just across the street. Mummy assured me that the children would be asleep, and I could do my homework or read. If anything came up, all I had to do was call the school. That all sounded reasonable enough. Feeling flattered and grown-up, I agreed, having no idea of the responsibility I was agreeing to.

Being late fall, it was chilly as I climbed into the back seat while Mummy sat in front, beside Daddy in the driver's seat. I tried to hide my apprehension as Daddy drove into the Rogers' driveway and parked the car. I looked out the window, estimating how far it was to Milliken School. *It can't be more than fifty yards. I could run over there if I had to!* No one had mentioned what to do in case of a fire. Or what to do in any emergency for that matter. Dad said they would wait in the car while I went inside.

I brought my bag with homework and *Kon-Tiki*, a book

I was thoroughly immersed in, and knocked on the door. Jay met me, standing barefoot in the hallway, casually dressed in a long skirt and sweater. She asked me to follow her upstairs, tiptoeing, to see where the children were sleeping. All was quiet, and I hoped it would remain so for as long as I was there.

I followed Jay back downstairs where she showed me how to heat the bottle of milk for Robin and how to test it on my arm to make sure it wasn't too hot. She said that I'd only need to heat the bottle if Robin cried. Then she said, in a vague sort of way, how to change Robin's diaper. Jay, known for being casual, didn't seem the least concerned that I had never changed a baby's diaper. I, on the other hand, was beginning to panic at the thought of having to lift Robin, move her to the diaper changer and actually change her diaper.

I must have appeared outwardly calm because Jay glanced at her watch and announced that she had to leave right away or be late for the PTA meeting. As she slipped on her loafers and a corduroy jacket, Jay reminded me that Milliken School's telephone number was posted with a brief list of other numbers on a table beneath the wall phone in the hallway. Ray put on his jacket, gave me a big smile and opened the door in time to meet up with Jay and my parents who were visibly anxious to get to the meeting. On time. No one looked back when I waved from inside the front door.

In the kitchen I caught a glimpse of a drawing on the wall. I'd noticed it earlier but I'd been so focused on how to heat the baby bottles, I hadn't taken a closer look. *Now I had plenty of time*. The cartoon-like drawing had been created for Ray and Jay's wedding and signed by the artist.

I'd never seen a drawing quite like this: simple with exaggerated features that captured the essences of Ray and Jay. This caricature was nothing like Mummy's exquisite drawings of animals.

It occurred to me, while in the kitchen, that this would be a good place to do my homework, so I tiptoed into the hallway to retrieve my bag, then sat down at the table. I glanced at my watch; they'd been gone for eight minutes. *Only eight minutes!* It was going to be a long night!

I was working on my homework when I heard a whimpering upstairs. *Please, please don't let it be Robin waking up!* I quietly inched to the bottom of the stairs and listened. Silence. I looked at my watch. They'd now been gone twenty minutes. No further sounds from upstairs. Relieved, I tiptoed back to the kitchen.

By the time I'd finished my homework an hour and ten minutes had gone by. *Please, oh please, may the children stay asleep.* They should be home any time now. I went to the window. No sign of them yet. *Hurry up! Come home! Please!*

Reading *Kon-Tiki* helped time go by. I was hoping to finish the chapter before the PTA meeting ended. Then, was I hearing voices? I looked at my watch. Laughter. No one had a laugh quite like Ray's. My first babysitting job was coming to an end, and it couldn't come fast enough.

I put my homework and *Kon-Tiki* back in my drawstring bag, prepared to leave as soon as they came through the door. Not wanting to wake the children, they opened the door and entered so quietly I wouldn't have heard them—had I not been awaiting their return from the moment they left. Maybe they were as anxious as I was since they asked if there were any problems. Did Brian stay asleep? Did Robin need to be fed?

I was happy to report that Robin had whimpered just once and that when I listened from the bottom of the stairs, all was quiet; as far as I could tell, Brian hadn't awakened at all. I didn't bother to tell them that I had been in panic mode from the moment they'd left, worried that I might have to feed Robin a bottle or change her diapers.

Ray and Jay thanked me effusively having no idea how relieved I was to be leaving.

Alice and Nardo, 1940

Fourth of July

I couldn't wait for the Fourth of July parade with the high school band led by high-stepping majorettes and floats fashioned by local businesses and organizations like the Girl Scouts, Porter Grange and Kiwanis Club. Along the parade route some children waved American flags while others covered their ears to block the sound of car horns blown in celebration of the holiday.

In seventh grade I got to be on a float with my friend Judy. Our float, a wagon poorly disguised as a lake, was pulled by a tractor that bore no resemblance to a motor boat. Hay bales covered with white sheets, adorned with waves of blue crepe paper, were at the back of the float; we stood on those bales, leaning back in our swimsuits and waving with one hand while holding the "tow ropes" secured at the front of the wagon. Onlookers along the sidewalks waved back as we basked in our heady moment!

Later in the afternoon there were softball games, picnics and social gatherings. Once the sun had set, people arrived in droves to stake out their viewing spots for the fireworks display, laying their blankets on the grassy knoll behind Porter High School. Children of all ages played tag, chased one another, squealed, shrieked, teased and even cried when their play got too rough, but they quickly recovered.

The Fourth of July was a true community affair, a time when people came together to celebrate the signing of the Declaration of Independence, granting the thirteen colonies independence from Great Britain in 1776. Our family celebrated the Fourth of July in traditional ways with family and friends.

We didn't have firecrackers but once it got dark Daddy gave us each a ten-inch sparkler to hold so he could light them with a match. Holding our lit rods tightly, we waited impatiently as they burned down until suddenly, sparks flew. Standing far apart we made swooping motions, creating our own light show. "Write your name in the air!" I shouted.

Our sparkler display was, to me, nearly as exciting as the public fireworks themselves because I got to hold the source of the sparks—right in front of me—until it burned out.

Christmas Eve

Icicles hung from the roof of the Kezar Falls Movie Theater, a two-story squarish building with a hip roof, built in 1884 and recently renovated. Inside, it was framed in dark brown wood with walls painted a light tan. A plush, maroon velveteen fabric covered the shiny wooden seats.

The theater was a favorite place for parents to leave their children on a Saturday afternoon for a few hours of escape and occasional mischief. For both. Dottie sat at the cash register in the darkened hallway with large rolls of tickets in red, green and yellow. Tickets for the matinée were a quarter. With each purchase Dottie tore the ticket in half, kept one half and gave the other to the customer as proof of payment. A narrow stairway rose to the mezzanine balcony where older kids went to "make out." I was curious to see what went on in the "passion pit"—as it was affectionately known—but I didn't have the nerve to venture up those stairs until a few years later.

It was Christmas Eve and Dad had dropped Kathy, Louise and me, along with our friends, Bill and Martha, off at the movie theater for the special Christmas Eve Program featuring cartoons and a movie. We each had 40 cents, enough for admission and a bag of popcorn. As we made our way between the heavy maroon-colored drapes to find seating, we whispered and giggled with each other and our friends until we settled, on a side row, toward the front.

Rumor had it that mice scurried along the floor eating popcorn. I kept watching excitedly until the lights went out, never mentioning anything to my sisters or Bill and Martha, but I secretly hoped to catch a glimpse of some rodent activity.

Once the lights went out the only light was the exit sign to the left of the stage. Suddenly, a burst of brass and kettledrums sounded from the speakers; action was about to begin! We sat, rapt, as the screen came to life with Bugs Bunny, Road Runner and Wile E. Coyote.

When the movie ended, dim lights guided us to the lobby. It was gently snowing as we stepped into the cold, dark though it was only 4:30 in the afternoon. Being Christmas Eve, excitement was in the air.

Dad, parked nearby, stepped out of the car, waving to catch our attention. We girls got into the back seat, while Bill sat up front with Dad. We were eager to get home to supper followed by singing Christmas carols.

We passed Goodwin's Store and the Methodist Church where the Christmas tree in the triangle shone with multi-colored lights. Throughout the village and along the river lights twinkled through the falling snow, adding to the wonderment. The roads were slippery and we were noticeably quiet on the ride to North Parsonsfield where Bill and Martha lived. Once they had been dropped off Dad was backing out when he noticed a figure walking along the edge of the road. He wondered aloud who it might be on this cold and snowy night.

As the figure came toward us it appeared to be a

middle-aged man in a fedora and long woolen coat. Dad waited until the man was within earshot and rolled down the window, asking if he could help. The man was traumatized and speechless. He couldn't reveal who he was or why he was walking on this country road. Dad asked if he needed a ride, and without speaking, he got into the passenger's seat, staring straight ahead. He closed the car door, and Dad tried, unsuccessfully, to find out who he was and where he might be going. Meanwhile we sat in the back wondering what would happen next.

"Dad, why didn't you turn onto our road?" I asked.

Instead of heading home we were on our way to Cornish, about four miles away. Dad explained that he was going to put the stranger up for the night at the New Lincoln Hotel where he'd be fed and, hopefully, remember who he was and why he was here at Christmastime.

On the way home Dad helped us understand that this stranger likely suffered from amnesia—maybe a war trauma. *How could he forget who he was? Why would he be out on a back road on Christmas Eve?* I still wonder. I could tell how moved Dad was; his random act of kindness touched me deeply.

We got home in time for supper—to sing Christmas carols, and to listen to Bing Crosby sing "White Christmas." Before bed we put out a glass of milk and a cookie for Santa Claus, got ready for bed and then went to Louise's room where Mummy read us the story of the nativity. It was a favorite family time.

Every Christmas since then, I've thought of Dad's kindness on that snowy Christmas Eve, so many years ago.

Greeting Adolescence with a Bang

Hunting is a way of life in rural Maine, and most hunters I have known remained committed to old values like getting permission from the landowner whether their land is posted or not, fully knowing the territory where one is intending to hunt and firing as few shots as possible.

My parents came to Maine from Massachusetts in 1940 and did not share in the long-held hunting tradition. Having grown up in the small Massachusetts town of Sherborn, Dad was sensitive to our rural community, to hunting and its local traditions, so he only posted our property after a high school student unintentionally shot through our house as he hunted along the roadside, just after daybreak.

Everyone but Gram woke to the ear-piercing crack of the bullet passing through the exterior wall, then over the dining room table, cast-iron stove, and through the kitchen closet, finally lodging in insulation in the cellar way. Had Gram Hadlock not been sick in bed for the first time in seven years, she would likely have been standing over the stove in the very spot where the bullet passed through.

Dad, visibly upset, raced off in the direction from which the bullet had been fired. Unaware that he'd shot through our house, the young man was walking toward his car when Dad confronted him from his Jeep. The young man explained that there was a deer in the road right in front of him. He hadn't seen our house... and didn't even know it was there!

Dad told him where his bullet went, emphasizing how lucky he was that Gram Hadlock was sick in bed.

————

Dad seldom shot his .22-caliber shotgun—most often when a woodchuck feasted on tender green shoots or lettuce in the garden. One time I went to pick beans only to find a "mowed" line of green stubble. Not a bean in sight. For a brief time Dad went bird hunting for partridge when they were plentiful and in season. If he was succeeded, we got to enjoy a partridge feast from a recipe he'd adapted from Nonna. Dad's recipe called for marinating the plucked partridge in red wine, garlic and herbs for several days, then pan frying them in olive oil. Oh, the delectable aroma!

When my mother, sisters and I pleaded with Dad to let the woodchucks live he reminded us, "There's no point in having a garden if you have woodchucks living nearby. If you want woodchucks, you can kiss the garden goodbye."

We always had a garden.

————

When I was twelve I wanted a gun, even if it only shot caps. Practice shooting with Bobby behind the camp was such fun that I thought I'd like to shoot a cap gun, something that wouldn't be a threat to anyone, including me. Besides, I liked the rapid succession of BANGS possible with a cap gun.

"Please, may I have a cap gun? I'll be careful not to point it at anyone, even if it doesn't have bullets. After all, I shoot

Bobby's gun at the target behind his camp, and I'm very careful."

My parents glanced at one another in silence. Mom looked disgusted. She was generally opposed to guns but made exceptions for people who relied on hunting to feed their families.

"Well? May I?"

Finally Dad cleared his throat.

"You don't need a gun, honey. The only reason I have one is to keep woodchucks out of the garden."

There was no use badgering my parents about a gun, so I let the issue rest.

———

Just before my thirteenth birthday I brought up the gun issue again, only this time I was more subtle. When Mummy asked who I'd like to invite to my birthday, I replied, "Instead of going to the beach at Pine Point this year, I'd like to go to Norton's Hardware."

Mummy looked at me in disbelief. "Norton's Hardware? Why on earth would you want to go to Norton's Hardware on your thirteenth birthday?"

I wondered if I should say what was on my mind, and then it slipped out. "I'd like to choose something special to celebrate becoming a teenager. Dad, could I go downtown with you when you go to the bank? I know just what I want."

On the first day of August I drove to town with Dad. As he pulled up in front of the hardware store he asked, "Should I pick you up when I've finished my business at the bank, or would you rather meet me at the bank?"

With the door handle grasped in my right hand I looked

at Dad, "I'll use the money you gave me with my birthday card to get just what I want, then I'll come to the bank."

Although it was called Norton's Hardware they sold everything from hairnets and lipstick to toys and sewing notions in an annex to the hardware department. It took me only seconds to walk into the store, select the shiny pistol (that looked so real it almost scared me) and bring it to the cash register.

Mrs. Caston was the only person working that day. I'd had some minor run-ins with her as I used to go into the hardware department with my friend Lynn, and we'd giggle uncontrollably until Mrs. Caston asked us to leave. I pulled my wallet out of my pocket, and laid the money on the counter.

"Wait. I forgot to get some caps!" I dashed back to the toy aisle to grab a roll of caps.

"Do you have another two cents... for tax?" she asked. I looked in the change pocket of my wallet and found two more pennies. Mrs. Caston smiled. "Is this a present for someone?"

"It's a present for me!" She looked disapproving. This wasn't unusual, though. I had given her plenty of reasons to disapprove of my actions.

"For *YOU?!*"

"YUP," I answered proudly.

"Would you like a bag?" she asked. I took her up on her offer and hurried across the street to the car, parked in front of the bank. Dad had finished his business and was talking with Carl Hammond, who had come down from his jewelry shop to get his mail. My father talked with everyone he knew—even people he didn't know. *Oh boy. Now I'll have to wait—forever.*

As my patience wore thin, Dad finally told Carl that it was time to get home. He turned the key in the ignition to start the engine, and looked both ways before backing onto Federal Road.

"Did you find what you wanted, honey?" he asked.

I clutched the bag with my cap gun. "Wanna see what I bought?" I asked.

"Why don't you show me when we get home." *Do I have to wait all that time?*

Fifteen minutes later, as we drove into the driveway, I was exploding with anticipation. Gingerly, I opened the brown paper bag and drew out my long-awaited treasure. I raised my eyebrows and tried to anticipate his response.

"I guess if it's what you want, honey," he said matter of factly. He wasn't thrilled; that was obvious. But I sure was! Dad wasn't one to hide his emotions—ever. Neither was I! I raced into the house to find my sisters.

"Wanna play Cowboys and Indians out by the big rock?"

"Nah. Louise and I are playing with our dolls," Kathy replied. My sisters' lack of enthusiasm wasn't going to deter my plans. Across the field I ran, brandishing my shiny silver pistol in the air and caps in my pocket. As I came to the edge of the field I slowed down, crawled under the barbed-wire fence and raced to the big granite rock with mossy areas along the surface. *Perfect!* I scrambled to the top of the boulder, loaded the caps, and pulled the trigger. BANG! BANG-BANG-BANG-BANG! *Even better than I'd dreamed!* In less than five minutes I'd shot the entire roll of caps delighted by the mini-explosions and the alluring smell of sulfur.

Rev definitely wouldn't have approved of this diversion, and I had no intention of telling her. Although neither of my parents could understand why their thirteen-year-old daughter wanted a cap gun, they were willing to let me have the experience. No doubt they hoped that I'd soon relinquish my gun for something more "ladylike." I don't think I ever shot caps from my pistol again. In fact, it soon disappeared, and I never thought much about it again— only the smell of sulphur accompanied by loud bangs.

Having just become an official teenager, I was feeling conflicted and awkward.

Thirteen

Thirteenth birthday. I don't want to grow up or be a teenager—not today anyway. Dad said I could learn to drive when I turned thirteen. Would I rather play Cowboys and Indians or learn to drive? Now I can ride my bike to Cornish with Mary Lou. Her uncle has the Texaco gas station, and Mary Lou says he'll probably give us each a candy bar. I'm not sure I want to chase after boys, though. Except maybe Richard. He lives in Cornish and he's really cute. He calls me sometimes. Dad doesn't let me talk very long though. He says I must respect that we're on a party line—that others may need to use the phone. Actually, I like having Dad make me get off the phone because most of the time I'm really bored talking with Richard. I'd rather be making something... like a house in the woods or a potholder with Gram or a bow and arrows from maple saplings along the road. Mary Lou's birthday is the day after tomorrow. If I can get a ride to town we'll do something special. I know! I'll get a pack of cigarettes, and Mary Lou and I will take them to Spec Pond. If there are too many people there we'll go up to the cemetery behind her house to smoke.

Once every two or three months Mum went to Jen Kelly's Hair Salon to get a perm for her baby-fine hair. Though the perms were not flattering, Mum enjoyed being pampered by Jen, an elegant, stylish woman who always wore chic dresses and high heels. Those perms did a number on Mum's hair follicles—something she regretted for the rest of her life.

I hatched a plan to celebrate Mary Lou's birthday and wanted confirmation that it could work. "Mummy, since you're going to Jen Kel's tomorrow, would you drop me off at Mary Lou's while you're getting your hair permed?"

Mummy considered my question before responding. "You should be finished with your chores by 10 o'clock, so I don't see why not. I have to leave by 10:15 for my 10:30 appointment, but you should be ready by then."

"What time shall I plan on being picked up?"

"Maybe you'd better walk to Jen Kel's from Mary Lou's. I should be ready to leave by 2:30."

"Sure, I'll be there by 2:20—in case you're ready a little early." I said, being overly amenable.

That night I went to bed figuring out my strategy once Mummy dropped me off.

The following morning was bright and clear as we drove downtown. "What a lovely day! Not a cloud in the sky." Mummy exclaimed. "A weather-breeder."

"A what?" I asked.

"A weather-breeder," Mummy reiterated. "That's an expression for a clear, cloudless day like this one. Stormy weather is sure to follow."

As we drove on Route 25, alongside the Ossipee River, I was thinking ahead. "Mummy, why don't you drop me off at the church. It's just a short walk to Mary Lou's from there."

Mummy turned left and pulled up beside the sidewalk in front of the Methodist Church. I opened my door and got out, reminding her, "I'll be in front of Jen Kel's by 2:20."

Mummy waved goodbye as she pulled away. I watched her until she disappeared around the corner. Ridlon's Store was just across the street, and Jim Virtue's tired old horse and wagon was tied to the light post, shifting his feet to stay awake. I walked past the horse and into the store where Joe Ridlon was stationed at the cash register.

"What can I do for you, young lady?" *Be discreet. Act grown up.*

"I'd like a pack of Marlboros for my dad." I said. "He asked me to buy them for him."

Joe looked me squarely in the eye. "I'm pretty sure your dad didn't ask you to get Marlboros since he smokes Lucky Strikes. If he wants cigarettes, you should bring a note from him next time."

I was way too humiliated to argue, and I wouldn't have anyway. I was deeply uncomfortable telling a lie. I made a hasty retreat, running past Jim's horse, across the road and through the churchyard to Mary Lou's. Mary opened the door after I knocked. "Happy birthday... almost!" I said in a sing-songy way.

I was actually relieved to not have to smoke vile-tasting cigarettes. Instead, Mary Lou and I went to Ridlon's Pharmacy where we had chocolate ice cream cones with jimmies that tasted oh so GOOD! And I still had fifteen cents!

Mr. Crowley

Seventh grade looked ever so promising. Mr. Crowley, a recent graduate of Saint Anselm in New Hampshire, was to be the seventh grade teacher at Milliken School. His photograph, published in the local news section of the *Portland Press Herald*, made my friend Mary Lou and me swoon. A most welcome addition after seven years of women teachers!

The first day of school began as usual with the ringing of the bell followed by morning exercises: salute to the flag, the Lord's Prayer and a poem Mr. Crowley had chosen from his *Anthology of Poems*. As he read the poem I noticed a tooth on his lower jaw protruding, especially when he wasn't smiling—a defining feature, I thought, that made him look distinguished.

It took a while for Mr. Crowley to get used to our class and for us to get used to him. When he had a feeling the time was right, he introduced an activity he'd taken from one of his college classes: ask each student to write five sentences that describe someone in class.

Mr. Crowley scanned the descriptions before reading them. "Can anyone guess who this is," he asked. "This person is small... doesn't attend church... has pigtails... easily has the giggles and rides on the bus." No one had any difficulty identifying me.

What bothered me about this exercise was that some kids weren't described at all. After class I suggested to Mr. Crowley that he give everyone someone's name so everyone would be included. He followed through, and gave us the assignment again. All descriptions had to show kindness and respect. It was, I thought, better the second time around. As he wrote changes to the exercise on the blackboard, Mr. Crowley flipped his chalk as he described them, catching it most of the time, but when he didn't he bent over, picked up the chalk and stuffed it into his suit jacket pocket. *Too weird! Was his pocket full of chalk dust?*

At the end of the school day Mr. Crowley stood in the doorway of our classroom and called names of students as their buses arrived. While he was distracted, a few of us girls wrote notes on the blackboard, sometimes adding cartoon-like drawings and always accompanied them with uncontrollable giggles and side glances. As adolescents we were thrilled to have a male teacher who seemed to like us even though our hormones were unpredictable.

Feeling slightly under par one day, I carried my malaise a step further and feigned illness. I told Mr. Crowley I was feeling sick to my stomach, thinking there was a slight chance he might offer to drive me home—especially since he'd recently had dinner at our home, and he and Dad were striking up a friendship.

At the end of class Mr. Crowley beckoned me to his desk and said quietly, "If you're willing to wait twenty minutes I'll give you a ride home." I tried not to be too obvious. "Are you sure? Thank you, Mr. Crowley."

It had snowed intermittently throughout the day, and the roads were slippery. Mr. Crowley brushed snow from both sides of his gray Chevy before we climbed in. I was excited to be riding home with him, but also feeling painfully awkward. *What's going on? I shouldn't be doing this, but I can't stop now.*

We'd driven halfway up Hunt's Hill when the car began to slide, right off the ice-covered road. By this time I'd forgotten my illness and jumped out on the passenger side, determined that if I were to give a steady push against the bumper on my side, we'd get the car back on the road. Mr. Crowley reached across the seat to roll down the window on the passenger side. I called out, "If I push from this side, I'm pretty sure we can get the car out of the ditch."

"I thought you were sick," he said.

"I'm feeling much better now. I can walk home from here," I offered, brushing snow from my face.

Once the car was back on the road I got back in. Mr. Crowley assured me that he wasn't going to let me walk through blowing snow, on an icy road, even if I no longer felt sick.

When he drove into the dooryard, before I opened the door to get out, I said guiltily, "Thank you, Mr. Crowley. I'm so sorry for the trouble I've caused."

Dad came out to thank him while I dragged myself into the house.

Magazine Sales

In early November one of the leading magazine publishers sent out promotional packets to seventh-grade teachers. Part of the emphasis was on working together to out-perform other seventh grades around the country: one lucky class would win a weekend trip to Washington D.C. while the rest of would have to sell enough subscriptions to take a class trip. Mr. Crowley shared his skepticism with us.

Mr. Crowley offered two suggestions for where we might go: Benson's Animal Farm in Hudson, New Hampshire or White Lake State Park in Ossipee, New Hampshire. We voted to go to Benson's Animal Farm. Not only was it farther away, none of us had been there.

Each magazine was worth a certain number of points, and our goal was to sell as many magazines as possible to earn points for our trip. Mr. Crowley kept a flier at his desk with photos of prizes one could win by accruing enough points. For example, a subscription to *Farm Journal* was worth two points. *Arizona Highways*, a glossy publication with color photos of the Grand Canyon, Petrified Forest and colorful sunsets was 10 points! We kept a close tab on available prizes as we sold subscriptions.

———

The compact, in the shape of a miniature suitcase, was covered in red leather with college pennants embossed on the smooth red surface. I'd never used powder, and never would, but the prospect of owning something so grown-up was still enticing. This compact seems to have been consistent with my subscription to the *Ladies' Home Journal*, bought with my allowance and babysitting money. I was especially curious to read the question-and-answer section, along with cooking and the women's photography sections. (My family didn't eat like that!)

Another of my favorite reads was my mother's reference book, *The Child From Five to Ten*. It contained a section on what parents should expect from a "normal ten-year-old" that I referred to from time to time. Though I was two years beyond ten, it still helped me figure out whether I was developing "normally."

The other item I selected was a leather holster with a camping ax, a straight-blade knife and a flashlight. "You don't want a boy's camping holster!" Mr. Crowley chided, as though I'd not thought clearly about what it was I wanted. "Of course I do," I answered, embarrassed by having been confronted publicly about my choices.

In hindsight, the two items I chose reflected my struggle with becoming a teenager and represented the woman I became.

Hornpoutin'

A star-filled evening on Bickford Pond is among my favorite memories. A small group of us gathered at the Mouton's camp to climb aboard Bobby's wooden boat as the lights came on, one by one at the end of the pond. Bobby, standing with one hand on the starter, looked for the best route to the fishing hole to avoid getting tangled in lily pads. He brushed his nose with his free hand then pulled the starter.

"We're off," he said, pushing the lever forward. "We haven't far to go, just thirty-five to forty feet before we get to the deepest part of the cove. In fact... we're here!" He cut the motor and shouted, "I'm about to drop anchor, so duck if you don't want to get wet!" The anchor plunged into the water, sinking to the bottom. Bobby wound the anchor rope around a brass cleat on the stern. Points of light appeared in the night sky until darkness overtook us, and the sky was peppered with stars. A bat swooped overhead. Then another and another. Being on the pond at dusk was magical.

Bobby, not being shy, said, "Someone hand me the bait can. It's metal with holes on top. Let me know if you need help baiting your hook. Nightcrawlers can be wiggly little suckers when you try to grab hold of one!"

Our wooden hand lines, shaped like three-dimensional

tic-tac-toes with the fishing line wrapped around the middle, were useful for catching hornpout. When we freed our hooks, Bobby extended his arm with the open bait can. "Go ahead, take one, they won't bite, but boy can they wiggle!" he said gleefully, knowing how squeamish some were at the thought of touching nightcrawlers or worms of any kind.

Holding my hook between my thumb and forefinger of my left hand, I tentatively reached into the can Bobby patiently held, trying to remain calm as I felt for a crawler, but the slimy textures wiggling in the can gave me the willies. "These worms give me the creeps! Bobby, I give in. Will you bait my hook? Please!"

Seconds later Barbara yelled, "I can't hang on to this darned thing! Oh! No! " She flung her arm, attempting to fling the worm back into the bait can. Instead the worm wriggled beneath the floorboards. "Don't worry about a wiggly worm," Bobby chortled. "There are plenty more where that one came from."

By this time he was holding all the hand lines, baiting them while Harv was in the bow attaching a shiny lure to his pole line. "Hey, buddy, you think this will work?" Harv asked.

Bobby joked, "Only one way to find out, Harv!"

Harv replied, "It'll work or it won't."

"There you go, Harv. You sound like a philosopher... or a scientist!" Bobby laughed, pleased with his observation.

The night sky was the evening's magnum opus. It elicited reflective thoughts amongst us all. Bobby dominated the discussion, talking incessantly about planets, stars, northern lights and the Milky Way while meteors streaked across the sky. We searched for constellations and marveled at the universe, conjecturing its origins and what its future might hold.

On glorious evenings such as this, Bobby would often become philosophical as we cast our gazes upward. This time, though, he veered off track and ended up telling questionable stories on the invasion of our solar system—even our country—by aliens. We listened, stifling giggles. "Where do you get your information, anyway?" I finally asked.

"I have my sources," Bobby answered wryly. "Anyone can read about the flying saucer that landed in Roswell."

The magnificence of the evening was transformed when Barbara could no longer accept Bobby's far-fetched stories and exploded with laughter. "Bobby, you don't believe everything you read, *do* you?"

Bobby answered in a serious tone. "Since the UFO crashed in Roswell, there's a serious threat to our country. I could tell you more, but I don't want to scare you. Besides, this information is top secret." He smiled broadly.

"Then why are you sharing this information?" I asked. "I agree that spaceships are possible, but you don't have any way of getting hold of "top secrets.'"

The magic of the night was temporarily lost... until we stopped arguing and looked up.

"I think something's biting!" Kathy said excitedly. Bobby reached for her line. "Yup! You have a good-sized 'pout here." He handed the hand-line back to her so she could slowly reel in the line. "Remember not to grab at the pout or you'll be sorry," he reminded.

Kathy handed the line back to Bobby. "Will you bring the pout in and take it off the line?"

Bobby hauled in the pout and cautiously tossed the

slippery fish into a small tub with the evening's catch; he re-baited Kathy's hook and handed it back to her.

Again, staring into the night sky, Bobby observed, "Tonight we have a great view of Cassiopeia. Can you find it?" He pointed to the bright stars forming a "W" in the northern sky.

"All I can find is the Big Dipper," Barbara giggled. "Besides, as long as Cassiopeia is still up there, it doesn't really matter if I can find it... does it?"

"Don't give up so easily," Bobby said. "You never know... knowing a constellation might come in handy someday."

The Letter

It was early spring of 1954. Remnants of snow banks still lined the roads in Kezar Falls. I was one of sixteen students in eighth grade, in a classroom housed at the local high school. Our teacher, Mr. True, was called "Pinky" by most townspeople, including his basketball team, but I just couldn't bring myself to call him that to his face. It seemed disrespectful.

Those of us who didn't bring a bagged lunch from home would walk about a mile, across the bridge to Parsonsfield, to eat hot lunches at Milliken School. I always regretted not having brought my lunch when one of the more unappetizing meals, tuna or salmon wiggle, was being served in a creamy sauce with peas, carrots and chunks of whatever wiggle it was, served on crackers. Moose stew, consisting of potatoes, carrots and flannel-like strings of meat from moose hit by motor vehicles wasn't particularly appetizing either; but worst of all were the blue-green eggs in creamed sauce akin to a wiggle. That was a hard meal to swallow!

Each day, Stacey's Farm delivered crates of pasteurized milk in half-pint, glass bottles to the back entry of Milliken School. At noon the milk was distributed, along with hot lunches, to students, even if the milk had soured after sitting too long in the sun. We were, nevertheless, expected to eat everything on our plates and to leave no milk in the bottles.

As Judy, Lynn, Mary Lou and I walked across the bridge and back, we noticed a man who, during the mill's lunch break, stood each day on the bridge, reading his newspaper, never looking up to see who was passing by. His routine never wavered. On a day that Barry, a friend and classmate, had to leave early for lunch, he reported seeing the man coming from the woolen mill after the noon whistle. That whistle could be heard all over town, announcing lunch time in Kezar Falls. People in town knew one another, but no one seemed to know who this stranger was.

Girls at thirteen can be catty, and I was no exception. Lynn sometimes became agitated over circumstances that seemed to me fairly trivial; the stranger on the bridge seemed to me a credible reason for her heightened anxiety. As we walked back from Milliken School I caught up with Lynn.

"Lynn, do you have any idea who the stranger on the bridge could be?"

She'd obviously given this question more than a little thought. "I'm pretty sure he's a Communist spy," she answered solemnly.

"What makes you think that?" I asked.

"Because he doesn't act like anyone else," Lynn replied.

"But this is Maine. Why would anyone want to spy on this little community?" It was true, though. He didn't act like other townspeople; his behavior was different.

The McCarthy hearings stirred up strong sentiments across our nation, and Kezar Falls was no exception. My parents, who usually limited their weekday television viewing to the evening news, watched the hearings whenever they could. I watched as long as I'd finished my chores and homework. I noticed that my parents' facial expressions were often troubled. They spoke with each other, in front of me, of their concern for people being summarily persecuted by Senator Joseph McCarthy.

I watched the proceedings with intensity, grasping to understand the fear being instilled in the public arena. Until I had a better understanding of what was happening I was ambivalent, mostly out of ignorance. But when I learned that some of my favorite celebrities, including Leonard Bernstein, Lena Horne and Kenneth Roberts, were on the "blacklist" of the House Un-American Activities Committee, I better understood my parents' concerns that everyone was affected by this "witch hunt," directly or indirectly.

The night following my exchange with Lynn, I started thinking how far-fetched it was to think that a Communist was standing on the bridge, spying on people in our town. Lynn was confirming McCarthy's paranoia: that we were victims of a subversive plot. This was so presumptuous that I had to do something! I devised a scheme that could be accomplished in a few minutes. The following day, at noon recess, I shared my thoughts with Mary Lou. She liked my idea—thought it was worth doing. I hoped we could pull it off before the buses loaded.

When I glanced at the clock on the classroom wall it was only five minutes before the last bell. My classmates and I created a small commotion as we gathered up our books to wait for the buses that would bring us home. I had just enough time if I hurried. I scrawled a note with my left hand on a piece of yellow-lined paper:

Meet me behind the office of the woolen mill tomorrow night at 7:00 or your life will be in danger. Sincerely, the man on the bridge

I slipped the note into a regular-sized envelope I'd brought from home. As my classmates put on their coats and hats, talking with each other, I wrote Lynn's address on the envelope, licked the flap and rubbed it shut. I signaled to Mary Lou to come by my desk.

"I got it written! Would you mail this after school if I give you five cents for the stamp?" Mailing a letter cost three cents.

"I'm going to the post office anyway and will drop it off when I pick up my mail," she smiled. Before I handed her the letter I rubbed the envelope on the seat of the chair next to mine to make it look sinister. Then I took lipstick from my cosmetic case and rubbed it on the back flap of the envelope—to look like blood. Mary Lou took the letter, and I got on the bus as it was about to leave.

I waved to Mary Lou as I watched her leaving with the letter in hand. On the way home I did a few math problems and made small talk with friends. By the time I got off the bus I'd forgotten all about the letter.

The next morning I was looking forward to seeing Mr. True and my classmates, but when I stepped inside the school building I realized something was very wrong. Mr. True and other teachers huddled in the hallway, all with looks of consternation. *Why were seniors in our eighth grade classroom? What was going on?*

When Mr. True came toward me, I asked, "What's all the commotion about?"

"You haven't heard?"

"Heard what?"

Mr. True moved back to the hallway and asked me to come with him. He leaned toward my ear and said in a near whisper, "Did you by any chance receive a letter in the mail yesterday?"

It slowly occurred to me what was going on. *Oh no!*

"Y-e-es, YES," I lied.

"Don't worry," he said. The FBI has been called. They're sending someone to investigate. They'll be here this afternoon." *FBI? This was getting way too serious!*

Mr. True continued, "Lynn's grandmother, Mrs. Griffith, had a bad heart spell after seeing the letter and had to have the doctor come see her last night." Lynn's grandparents shared the house with their two daughters, their husbands and six grandchildren.

"How awful!" I exclaimed. "Is she okay now?"

"I think she's okay, but having Lynn receive that letter was very upsetting, as you can well imagine."

After carefully thinking it over I knew that telling the truth was where Mary Lou and I had to begin. When the first bell rang I signaled her to come downstairs with me. She followed me into the boiler room. Panic-stricken I exclaimed, "Mary Lou, we have to tell Mr. True what really happened. Right away!"

She wasn't convinced.

"We must! It's the only thing we can do unless we want to face the FBI!"

"Will you do the talking?" Mary Lou asked timidly.

"I will," I answered emphatically.

"C'mon, we don't have much time! We've got to hurry!" We raced upstairs. "Where's Mr. True?" I gasped, glancing around the room.

"He's on the phone," a student replied. The bell rang

and students moved to their next class. I tried to be as inconspicuous as I could, through the crowded hallway, to join Mary Lou, standing in the doorway of the principal's office. As soon as Mr. True hung up the phone, I blurted in desperation, "We have to speak with you, right away!"

Mr. True didn't seem to react with much concern—maybe because I was the anxious one.

"What's on your mind?" he asked.

I swallowed awkwardly. "Mr. True, I... wrote... the... letter and... Mary Lou mailed it for me."

His face reddened. "You're telling me the truth—not making this up?"

"Yes! I am... I wouldn't lie!" I lied.

"Whatever made you do something like that?" he asked. "I'll call your folks right away; then I'll call Lynn's. You girls go back to class for now." Mr. True shook his head from side to side in disbelief. *What about the FBI? Who'll call them so they won't come? I imagined the agents in their overcoats and fedoras, arriving from Washington D.C., carrying their briefcases.* Momentary fear gripped me as I headed back to class.

A substitute teacher was working with our class on a math problem when Mary Lou and I were called back to Mr. True's office. There to greet us was Mr. McDaniel, rheumy-eyed, long-time postmaster at the Kezar Falls Post Office, wheezing, overweight and so lame he walked with great difficulty. He looked me in the eye through his wire-rimmed glasses.

"I can't believe you sent a threatening letter, but I'm sure you didn't mean any harm." He dabbed at his cheeks with his handkerchief where tears collected beneath his lower lids. He continued to speak gently, without judgment, but wheezing all the while. I worried he would suffer a heart attack right in front of me. He seemed so concerned that this was something I must learn from, something I must never, ever do again.

I felt deep remorse, but mostly because Mr. McDaniel was so upset.

He looked at Mary Lou. "You mailed the letter and that's a felony, but I don't believe you were the instigator." A slight smile crossed his parched lips. "You go on back to your class. And next time, don't do something you know you shouldn't do!" Mary Lou walked out the side door leaving Mr. McDaniel and me looking at each other. *Now what? My heart raced, fearing the worst. I had no idea what a felony was, but I'd find out when I went home.*

Mr. McDaniel stared at me, then shifted his glance toward the door. When I turned to see what he was looking at, there stood my Dad. He came toward me, put his arm around my shoulders while he thanked Mr. McDaniel.

"Thank you for helping this young lady learn from her mistake," Dad said. "I'm pretty sure she won't do something like this again." Mr. McDaniel shook Dad's hand as he shuffled to leave.

"I'm pretty sure you learned a big lesson," he said, patting the top of my head, moving slowly past me.

What I'd done so innocently still didn't feel serious, but considering the disruption it caused, it obviously was. When we were alone I asked Dad what a felony was.

He thought for a moment, then answered. "It's a very serious offense. Usually a felon is sent to prison for quite a long time. You probably won't be going to prison, but things could have turned out a lot worse. You've got to learn to think ahead... think how your actions could affect others."

Dad seemed uncomfortable—maybe because, under similar circumstances, he might have been tempted to do something similar. He was forever telling adventurous stories of his youth involving daring and bravado, ending with a wise adult giving him counsel.

"Honey, why don't you go back to your class now. Then at noon recess explain to Mr. True that you're going to be leaving with me to go to the Griffith's. They want you to come for lunch. It's important for them and for you. You must apologize to them... and, of course, to Lynn."

I'd spent nights at the Griffith's triplex. I was especially fond of Mr. Griffith. He was so dignified and commanded respect from community members of all ages. Now in his late seventies he walked a few yards to the Post Office, but he mostly he stayed at home with Mrs. Griffith. She had difficulty moving around and spent most days sitting in her easy chair with her feet elevated. The Griffiths were a devoted couple who lived modestly after their years of work at the woolen mill. Mr. Griffith was active in the community, coaching prize speaking and teaching Sunday School at the Methodist Church.

When Dad drove up in front of their house a knot formed in the pit of my stomach. My heart pounded. "Dad, I'm not hungry. I don't think I can eat anything."

"Do the best you can, honey. The Griffiths are such good people, this has been hard on them. Eat what you can and you'll feel better."

I opened the car door, looked back at Dad and slowly got out. Before closing the car door behind me, I turned and leaned in. "Thank you, Dad."

As I walked toward the house, Mr. Griffith came to meet me. He reached out with his arms outstretched. I walked into his embrace feeling so ashamed and so thankful for his forgiveness. "Zippy, you run along into the house," he said, continuing toward Dad who had gotten out of the car. "Mrs. Griffith is waiting for you. I'll be right along." I couldn't hear what Mr. Griffith and Dad said to each other, but I was pretty sure I knew what it was about.

Hesitating to walk into the Griffith's alone, I waited in the outer hallway, trying to anticipate what would happen when I stepped inside. The front door slowly opened as Mr. Griffith pushed against the thumb latch. Holding onto the door jam he brushed his moccasins against the floor mat. His long white eyebrows moved expressively, synchronized with his facial expressions as he smiled at me warmly. His breathing was audible, like the gentle chuffing of a distant steam engine. With shallow breaths I followed him into their apartment.

There was a moment of silence when Mr. Griffith went into their bedroom to leave his jacket. Mrs. Griffith moved slowly, side to side, through the kitchen door into the living room. She concentrated on her every step and didn't seem to notice that I was standing by the living room door. "I'm very sorry," I said softly, hoping not to scare her.

I was truly sorry that I'd caused them such anxiety, that Mrs. Griffith had needed to have the doctor come. "I guess I didn't think about anything except pulling a prank on Lynn."

Mr. and Mrs. Griffith both wore somber expressions as he broke the tension by announcing, "Lynn's going to be joining us for lunch. She was pretty frightened last night, but she's better now. Say, why don't you take off your coat and leave it on the chair by the window." I took off my jacket and laid it on the chair.

Mrs. Griffith placed four pink placemats, stamped and cutout to resemble lace, on their kitchen table. "I hope you like corn chowder." Enthusiastically I answered, "It's one of my favorites." Mr. Griffith pulled a folding chair from behind the sideboard in the living room.

"Young lady, you have a seat right here!" As I was about to sit down Lynn came through the living room into the kitchen. At first I didn't know how to respond. We looked at each other, sheepishly. Then I reached out to give her a hug.

"Lynn, I'm so sorry! I had no idea what I was doing when I wrote the letter. It was supposed to be a joke!" She stifled a whimper and hugged me back. "I was pretty scared," she said.

"Soup's on!" Mr. Griffith announced jovially. Mrs. Griffith brought bowl by bowl of hot corn chowder to Mr. Griffith, who, in turn, set each one on a placemat.

"Lynn, you sit over there, and you, Zippy, sit over here by me, where I can keep my eye on you!" This comment made me smile. Mr. Griffith had my number. When we were all seated Mr. Griffith bowed his head and gave thanks for having us all together to share in the corn chowder Mrs. Griffith had prepared.

Amen.

Manny's Death

The sun was comforting as I sat atop the snowbank in front of the barn. I was twelve and my world had just shattered; I didn't know what was to become of me. Manny had been a part of my life since birth. It had been only a day since Manny and I had taken a short walk to the pine plantation, his first time out of bed for more than a brief trip to the bathroom, in three months. He let me know that he didn't have much time left and laid out his expectations for my life, including that I must never cut my braids.

Earlier that late January day in 1954, while we were eating lunch, Rev had burst through the front door with her boots still on, "Dear Manny has suffered a cerebral hemorrhage. As I headed out the door he asked that I not be gone long." His last words to me were, *'Ne soit pas longtemps, Cherie.'* Rev had walked to our house to ask for help. She was distressed but maintained her composure, "Alse, would you call Doctor Ridlon. I must get home right away."

Three months earlier, in November, Manny had an aneurysm that left him debilitated. At the urging of Doctor Ridlon, Rev rented a hospital bed. However, the only door the bed would fit through was the door to their summer kitchen, an uninsulated room, above a crawl space. That room's greatest advantage included a bank of windows facing south and two large west-facing windows, allowing the winter sun to warm and brighten the room—except, of course, when there was no sun—which was most of the time on either side of the winter solstice. Most of the wall space was lined with books, giving the room the warmth of "old friends," as Rev referred to them. Adjacent to the summer room, in a corner, was the bathroom with a chemical toilet and a few books on a small table in the already cramped space.

In her late sixties, Rev needed the height and flexibility of positions the hospital bed provided in order to care for Manny's incapacities. Throughout the winter she tended to his every need. Bedridden and delusional, he frequently imagined the nearby stone walls as infantry marching relentlessly to war.

Rev kept firewood stacked in a corner to feed the voracious wood stove in the summer kitchen. In addition, she kept the downstairs of the main house heated with a small cookstove where she prepared their simple meals. There was no plumbing, electricity or central heating, and Rev drew her water from a well behind the house. She had help from a local boy who came weekly to bring in firewood and water. When that ran out, she either brought it in herself or asked me for help.

In less than a half-hour Louise noticed Rev once again coming toward our house. "Why is Revy coming back?" she asked. This time Rev entered slowly, closing the door quietly, her eyes reddened and moist. "Dear Manny has left us," she sobbed. Mummy gave Rev a hug before Rev turned to me. "Zippoo, would you walk back with me? Manny would want you to."

"I will," I said, feeling utterly disoriented.

Dad added, "If you don't mind, Rev, I should probably give Press Stanley a call." Press would want to know that Manny wanted to be cremated so he could make arrangements for the transport. Dad looked at me. "Honey, you go along with Rev. Mummy and I will be coming right along."

Rev and I walked along the snow-covered road with shadows from the pines sweeping at the sunlight. I was glad to be with Rev but was confused and distraught. I felt strangely alone though Rev was right by my side.

I'd never seen a dead body before and was somewhat apprehensive but not afraid. Rev treated death as a part of life and helped me accept that Manny was prepared for death. He was no longer able to live as he wished or do any of the things that mattered to him. As we walked into the summer room I could see Manny's body lying on the bed, but Manny was no longer there.

I stood on my tiptoes to kiss his forehead. Revy sobbed, "He loved you so much, Zippoo." By this time, my composure was lost. Rev wrapped her long arms around me and hugged me snugly.

Mum and Dad came in as Rev and I were telling each other stories of Manny. Life was happening in slow motion when Dad broke the spell and asked Rev something that seemed to me very odd. He asked her if he could lay pennies on Manny's eyelids. "Dad, why would you want to put pennies on Manny's eyelids?"

"They weigh down the eyelids to keep them closed, like this," Dad said, laying a penny on each eyelid. *How weird.*

"Would you like some time alone with Manny before Press arrives?" Mum asked Rev. Tearfully, Rev agreed that she would, "I'd welcome that, dears."

Mummy, Dad and I walked slowly home, sharing memories.

Manny's death hit me hard. The following day my sisters and I drove to the Kezar Falls Post Office with Dad. They were ahead of me when I ran head-long into the Post Office door, oblivious to where I was or to what I was doing.

Haircut

I felt other-worldly for weeks after Manny's death, but slowly returned to my former self at home with the routines of daily life and at school. In the spring of my seventh grade year, I decided that I wanted to have my hair cut, to wear it short like my friends. I finally felt free to make my own choices about *my* preferences.

Girls in my class all had short, brown, light brown or dirty blond hair, permed, wavy or straight, and since my hair would never be blond or straight I figured at least I could have it short. This brought up a familiar question, one I frequently wrestled with, how much like everyone else did I want to be? Most of the time I liked being me.

On our way home from my transformative hair experience, I waited for Mummy to react to my new hairdo. Instead, she made small talk and didn't react at all. Perhaps she'd concluded that silence was preferable to a negative comment. Mummy was never one to say something she didn't mean.

Dad's reaction was another matter. I got out of the car as he was coming along the path from the henhouse. He looked incredulous as though he was seeing an apparition! "What in hell happened to you?" he asked, grimacing.

"What do you mean?" I asked. I hadn't paid much attention when Mrs. Flagg held the mirror for my approval after cutting off my braids. Afterward she placed aluminum clamps on either side of my head to create waves: two on one side and three on the other, while trying to convince me that my new look was "more suitable for a young lady." I certainly wasn't thrilled as I glanced in the large mirror. As I got out of the styling chair I had made a connection: my new hairdo would complement my recent subscription to *Ladies' Home Journal.* I was, after all, growing up, and how better to do it than with the guidance of the women's magazine with information on how to become an "All-American Woman."

I followed Mum and Dad into the house and headed straight for the bathroom to look at the new "me"—Dad's reaction was justified. My haircut was a disaster, but Mummy reminded me that hair grows, and I didn't have to have it cut again—unless I wanted to.

As it turned out, that haircut was the beginning of my being more assertive regarding choices that would ultimately define my sense of self. That fall, I would be attending high school at Fryeburg Academy. I was about to enter new territory, and my experiences, good and not so good, had prepared me to meet the challenge.

Charlotte, Kathy and Louise, 1953

Bobby and Zip

Gram Hadlock, Beauty and Louise

Rev and Charlotte

Charlotte and Josette

Curtis Chick

Louise, Kathy and Charlotte with Nardo

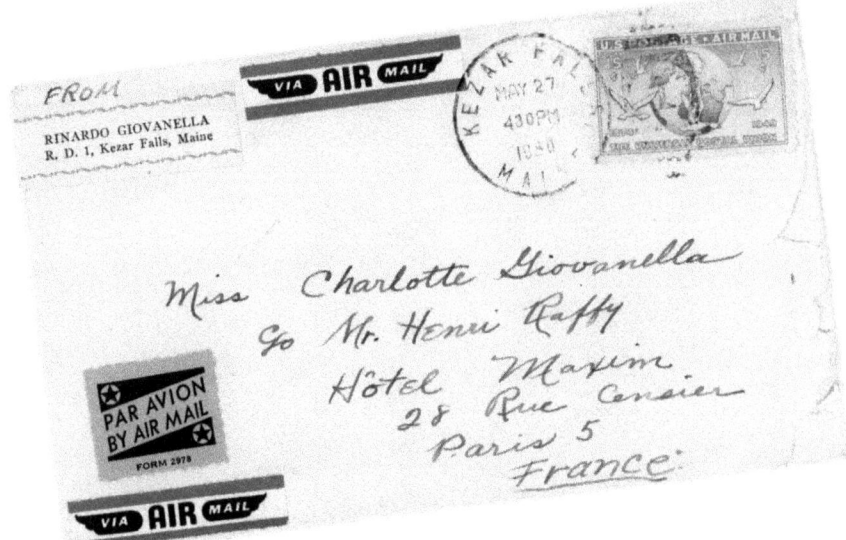

Acknowledgements

Everyone has a story to tell, and I am no exception. My family, along with the Raffys and my colorful neighbors were my initial inspiration for writing my recollections of the 1940s and early 1950s. Due to a lack of time and space I haven't included so many of you who helped me become who I am. I'm so grateful, and I thank each and every one of you.

Without the writing group I joined more than ten years ago, I wouldn't have undertaken these stories of my early childhood. I owe each of you my deepest gratitude. You've added a richness to my life that I couldn't possibly have foreseen. In alphabetical order, thank you, dear friends: Chris Chapman, Anne Wescott Dodd, Nancy Greenleaf, Kay Kavanaugh, Ann Kimmage, Jean Konzal, Eileen Landay, Heidi McGinley, Sue McCulley, Helen Regan and Carla Rensenbrink.

The support and encouragement from my sisters, Kathy Chaiklin and Louise Giovanella, initially prompted me to revisit the stories, accumulating in loose-leaf binders since I'd joined the writing group.

Editing and organizing were not something I could have undertaken alone. When I asked Jessica Esch, my friend and former student, if she knew of anyone I might contact for help compiling and editing my memoir, she furrowed her brow, pondered, then responded with an enthusiastic, "I think I'm that person!" Jess remembers saying, "I think you need me!" Both were true.

Without Jess, a positive, insightful catalyst in guiding me forward, this completed compilation of stories would not have happened.

Just when I thought I couldn't be more grateful for my good fortune, Jess suggested Anita Verna Crofts read the stories now compiled in book form. This meant that not only did I have the pleasure of having Jess as my navigator, Anita would be joining our team!

I couldn't be more thrilled to have Jess and Anita coaching me to the finish line. Thank you, my dears, for your expertise, your unwavering diligence and abundant good cheer! *Merci!*

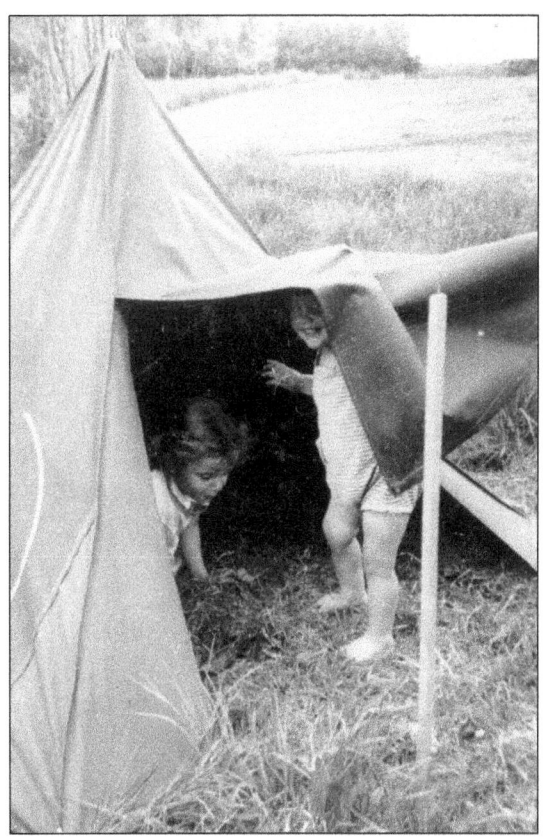

Charlotte and Kathy

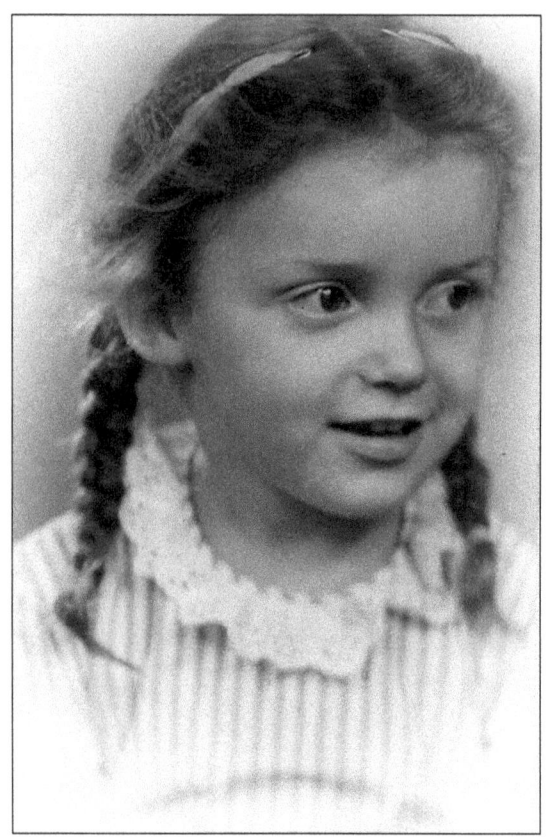

Charlotte, Age 4

Charlotte Giovanella Fullam was born in Portland, Maine in 1941 and lived much of her life in Porter where she grew up. An intrepid traveler from the age of four, she first crossed the Atlantic Ocean for a summer in France when she was eight. Trained as an arts educator, Fullam co-founded the New Country School in West Baldwin, taught art in Maine School Administrative District #55 and finished her teaching career at the University of Southern Maine in Gorham. She now lives on Munjoy Hill, overlooking the rising tides in Portland Harbor.

www.ingramcontent.com/pod-product-compliance
Lightning Source LLC
Chambersburg PA
CBHW051612120626
46551CB00014B/1757